Chinese Cuisine

Author: Huang Su-Huei
Editors: Chen Chang-Yen
Lai Yen-Jen
Gloria C. Martinez
Publisher: Huang Su-Huei
Wei-Chuan's Cooking
Dishes prepared by: Lee Mu-Tsun
Photographer: Aki Ohno
Designer: Ken Fukuda
Shaw, Haizan
Typesetting: Alton Litho Printers
Tung Chi Photo Typesting Co.
Printed by: International Scanner Colour
Separation Service, Inc.

ISBN-0-941676-10-2

Introduction

In writing Chinese Cuisine, published in 1972, I chose to use some of the simpler, more practical recipes introduced in our Wei-Chuan cooking classes. The book was so well received that additional editions were published in English, Chinese/English (bilingual edition), Japanese and French. Chinese Cuisine is still enjoying the same success it did in its early days. Many people are still discovering the wonders of Chinese cooking through this book and use it as a source of reference. Today's homemakers have come to look upon it as THE cookbook every home should have.

It was with the idea of bringing Chinese Cuisine into each and every home that I decided to publish the revised edition in hard and soft bound covers. The most up-to-date printing techniques have been used to ensure the clarity and overall high quality of the color prints in this book. The recipes have been tested several times to ensure their accuracy.

I hope you will continue to delight your family and friends with the delectable dishes presented here. I welcome any comments and recommendations regarding this book.

Chinese Cuisine

● Appetizers

● Chicken & Duckling

● Pork & Beef

● Fish, Shrimp & Other Seafood

● Bean Curd & Eggs

● Vegetables

• Soup

Culinary Idioms

Chinese cooking is a very subjective art. There are no definite quantities of any ingredients, nor any exact time limits for cooking any recipe. We encourage you to develop this art through trial and error. We have listed the basic information for the preparation of all dishes, as well as the ingredients needed; however, we encourage you to adapt the recipes to your own taste. In order that you may further understand the practice of Chinese cuisine, we give significant points and explain some expressions used often in Chinese cooking.

CLEANING

Clean the ingredients before using them, then drain and dry them thoroughly.

CUTTING

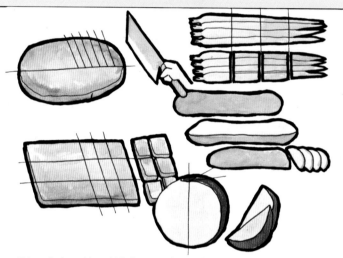

All ingredients must be cut into the same size and shape so that the cooked food will look uniform and have the same tenderness.

PRE-SEASONING

Chicken, pork, beef, fish, and shrimp must be marinated in the prescribed sauces to enhance the taste of the food. Coat with egg white then cornstarch to increase tenderness.

MIXING

If no cooking is required, just mix the ingredients together after cutting. If ingredients have been precooked, allow them to cool, then mix them together, add sauce and serve.

PRE-COOKING

Oil Out

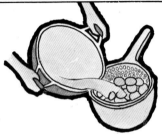

Place ingredients in hot oil or hot water for several seconds, or until slightly tender, then remove. (Pork, beef, chicken, fish, or Shrimp is usually sliced or shredded, seasoned, and coated with cornstarch before precooking.)

Preparing the wok:
Heat the wok then place 4 Tbsp. oil in wok and swirl it in wok to cover lower two-thirds of surface; remove excess oil. (This will prevent ingredients from sticking.)

Reheat wok and add enough oil to cover ingredients; heat oil until hot but not smoking. Add food. Stir quickly to separate ingredients; stir-fry until ingredients change color then remove. (Add 1 Tbsp. oil to ingredients and stir before frying. The ingredients will separate easily.)

STIR-FRYING

To put the material into a very hot wok over high heat and turn over and over until done.

Stir-frying is a very quick process. It is advisable to prepare all of the sauces in advance, including the cornstarch and water used to thicken the final sauce.

When several kinds of ingredients are used in cooking, the difference in tenderness of each ingredient will sometimes require that material be cooked in oil, boiled, or fried before mixing. Whichever method is used the ingredient must be precooked till tender.

When the preliminary preparation is finished, heat the wok and pour in oil. Add the onion, ginger root or garlic and stir until they impart their aroma. Add the ingredients, and a few drops of wine, if desired, to enhance the flavor of the food. Add the sauce and stir-fry until all ingredients are mixed together. This entire process must be short and quick so that the food will not overcook.

At this point, you may sprinkle a few drops of oil on the food. This will help to increase the brilliancy of the food and help to keep it warm.

STEAMING

To put the material in a steaming cage which is then put on a wok containing boiling water.

First, put water in the wok and allow it to come to a boil;

then place food in the cage and put it on the wok

Simple method for steaming: Place a bowl, upside down, on the bottom of the wok; add water (water should not cover the bowl). Put a heatproof plate on the bowl and place food on the heatproof plate, cover and steam

MIX-BOIL

First, put the sauce or soup into the wok by itself and allow it to boil, then add the food. The amount of cornstarch in the sauce should be to your own taste; however, there should not be too much sauce

STEWING

Stewing is similar to steaming. Put water in a large pot. Put material and water or stock to cover, in a smaller pot and set it inside the large pot. Cook over moderate heat until the food is tender. Soup prepared this way is very clear.

SMOKING

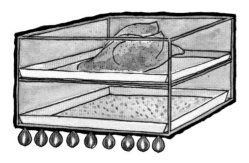

Put food in an oven (or cover and place on a grill); throw sugar, wood powder, or tea leaves into the fire or oven so that the fumes will smoke the food and give it flavor.

ROASTING

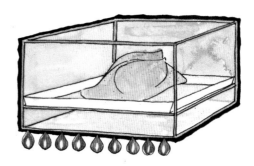

Cook or bake food in the oven with all the ingredients, until done.

DEEP-FRYING

To immerse the food in deep, hot oil.

Prepare the material for frying. The food must be marinated in the prescribed sauce, then coated with the proper flour or cornstarch batter.

There should be plenty of oil in the pan, enough to cover the material. However, if the material to be fried is very juicy or contains a lot of moisture, the oil should not occupy more than 60% of the wok so that it will not splash out of the wok.

First boil the oil; remove the wok from the heat and when the oil has cooled to medium temperature, put the food into the wok. Replace the wok over medium heat and cook until near-tender. Then turn heat to high and cook over high heat until done. This seals the flavor and ensures that the food will be completely cooked and crispy on the outside.

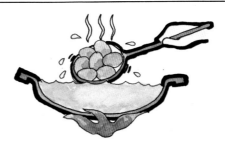

All food put into the oil at the same time must be removed at the same time to maintain uniformity.

STOCK

Broth from boiled pork, beef, or chicken meat or bones.

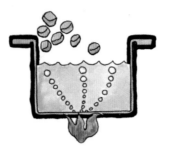

Boil water in a large pot, add pork, beef, or chicken meat or bones to boiling water. Remove. Discard water. (Purpose: to clean the meat.)

Put clean water in the pot and add the pork, beef, or chicken meat or bones. Bring to a boil and remove any scum. After removing scum, lower heat to medium. Add two green onions, two slices of ginger root, and one tablespoon wine. Cook for one hour. Remove pork, beef, or chicken. Stock is ready for use.

TABLE OF MEASUREMENTS

1 Cup (1 c.)
236 c.c.

1 Tablespoon (1 T.)
15 c.c.

1 Teaspoon (1 t.)
5 c.c.

Seasonings Used to Prepare Chinese Food

Five kinds of seasonings are frequently used to prepare Chinese food: salt, soy sauce, pepper, sugar, and sesame oil. Wine, vinegar, cornstarch, and oil for frying, etc., are also necessary.

Rice wine

Oil for frying

Sesame oil

Vinegar

Cornstarch

Soy sauce

Sugar

Salt

Black pepper

Utensils Used to Prepare Chinese Dishes

Cleavers, chopping block, spatulas, wok, and steamers are basic utensils used to prepare Chinese food A rolling pin, sifter, and wire whisk are also used to prepare Chinese snacks. An iron skillet or frying pan may also be used to cook chinese food. Roasting, frying, steaming, and stewing are cooking methods used to prepare a wide variety of delicious food.

Steamer

Wok

Strainer

Spatula

Cleaver

Sifter

Chopping Block

Wire Whisk

Rolling pin

VEGETABLES USED IN THIS BOOK

❶ Yellow Chinese Chives
❷ Coriander (Cilantro)
❸ Cauliflower
❹ Broccoli
❺ Chinese Broccoli
❻ Bok Choy
❼ Nappa Cabbage
❽ Cabbage
❾ Lettuce

❿ Chinese Celery
⓫ Celery

⓬ Lima Beans
⓭ String Beans
⓮ Green Peas
⓯ Soy Bean Sprouts
⓰ Snow Mung Bean Sprouts
⓱ Chinese Pea Pods

14

⓲ Canned Bamboo Shoots
⓳ Canned Young Bamboo Shoots
⓴ Canned Baby Corns
㉑ Canned Button Mushrooms
㉒ Pineapple
㉓ Green Onions
㉔ Brown Onions
㉕ Ginger Root
㉖ Fresh Garlic /Garlic Cloves

㉗ Hot Peppers
㉘ Green Bell Peppers
㉙ Winter Squash

㉚ Bitter Gourds
㉛ Cucumbers
㉜ Tomatoes
㉝ Eggplants
㉞ Water Chestnuts
㉟ Taro Root
㊱ Yams (Sweet Potatoes)
㊲ Potatoes
㊳ Daikon (White Radish)
㊴ Carrots
㊵ Gherkin Cucumbers

Description of and Instructions for some Special Ingredients

The ingredients for Chinese cooking encompass a wide range of foods. The most common ingredients are those readily available in markets: chicken, duckling, beef, pork, fish, shrimp, other sea foods, eggs, bean curd products, and vegetables We also use some dried foods. The dried foods include dainties of all lands and seas.

In this book, we have used the most commonly found ingredients. However, some famous dishes are regional and require special ingredients in order to obtain their original taste.

This section gives an explanation of the special ingredients and the methods to use and prepare them.

We hope you will understand this information easily and be able to use it properly.

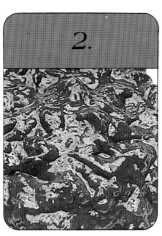

1.

2.

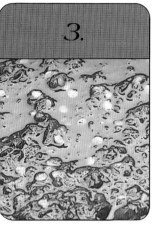

3.

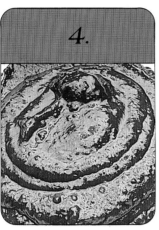

4.

5.

6.

7.

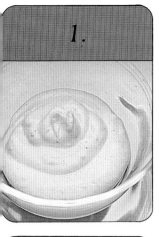

8.

❶ **Mustard Sauce:** Mix 1 Tbsp. dry mustard with 3/4 Tbsp. warm water; cover and let stand for 10 minutes. The sauce is yellow and becomes spicy. Dry mustard is made from the finely crushed seeds of the mustard greens.

❷ **Bean Paste:** Cook soy bean and wheat flour together; allow it to ferment. The bean paste is dark brown and will taste salty.

❸ **Hot Bean Paste:** Mix bean paste with chili paste. Chili paste may be substituted for hot bean paste.

❹ **Sweet Bean Paste:** This paste is made from fermented steamed bread. Sweet bean paste is black and very thick.

❺ **Fermented Black Beans:** cooked and fermented black beans that have been marinated in salty water. This bean is black and tastes salty.

❻ **Hot Red Pepper:** Dried hot red pepper.

❼ **Star Anise:** a fragrant spice used often in dishes cooked in soy sauce.
Szechuan Peppercorns: a spice used often in preparing Szechuan-style dishes.
Szechuan Peppercorn Powder: It is made from Szechuan peppercorns that have been stir-fried until fragrant and then ground to a fine powder.
Szechuan Peppercorn Salt: Stir-fry 1 Tbsp. salt in a pan until the salt is very hot. Mix with 1/2 tsp. Szechuan peppercorn powder. It can be served with fried chicken, fish, or shrimp.
Five-spice Powder: a combination of star anise, Szechuan peppercorns, cinnamon, fennel, and cloves that have first been stir-fried until fragrant and then ground to a fine powder.

❽ **Dried Scallops:** Before using, soak the dried scallops in hot water for 6 hours or add water to cover scallops and steam for 1 hour. Liquid may be retained for many dishes.

9.

10.

11.

12.

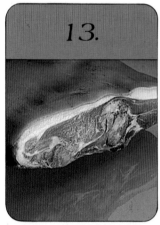

13.

14.

15.

16.

❾ Shark's Fin and Dried Fish Skin: There are two kinds of fins that are used, the dorsal fin and the ventral fin. The ventral fins are usually processed to make fin sheets. The dorsal fin must be prepared by soaking it in water overnight. Remove it from the water, tear off the skin and meat and discard them. Cook the remaining part (fin) in boiling water for 3 to 5 hours. Add water as needed to cover. When soft, the fin is ready to use. If fin sheets are used, soak them in hot water for 2 hours. Tear away the meat and skin from the fins. Cook the fin in boiling water for 1/2 hour or until soft; use. Dried fish Skin is soaked in water overnight. Remove and tear off the meat; discard. Cook in boiling water until soft.

❿ Bird's Nest: Swallows nests are found on seaside cliffs. They are built of seaweed and a certain secretion of the swallows. Choose a bird's nest that is white and has no feathers. Before using, soak it in warm water to cover for 4 hours. It will expand to 4 or 5 times its size and become soft. Remove then rinse to remove impurities and remove any remaining feathers; use. The bird's nest has no flavor so must be cooked in stock or used in a sweet soup.

⓫ Sea Cucumber (dried): Before using the sea cucumber, rinse to clean its surface. *Soak overnight. Discard the water; add clean water and bring to a boil; turn off the heat and let stand. When the water is cool, change the water and bring to a boil. Follow this procedure 3 times a day *for 2 days until the sea cucumber are soft. Use scissors to cut along the length of the bottom side (smooth side); remove all foreign matter and clean. Repeat from * for 2 more days. Total soaking time is 4 days. A large batch of sea cucumbers may be prepared in this manner and frozen and used when necessary.

⓬ Squid (dried): The squid used in the recipes in this book has already been reconstituted. To reconstitute the squid: Rinse the squid and soak it in warm water for 3 hours; remove and place it in baking soda water to cover (3 cups warm water and 2 Tbsp. baking soda); baking soda solution may be doubled. Soak for 6 hours; change the water 3 or 4 times during the soaking to remove the baking soda. When the squid has expanded, it is ready for use.

⓭ Chinese Ham: Use the whole pork leg; add salt and let stand for desired length of time. It is not unusual to marinate the ham for 6 months to 1 year. Cut off portions as needed. Cook portion to be used in water, green onion, ginger root, and wine. Remove and discard the broth and other ingredients. Cooked ham or Virginia ham may be substituted.

⓮ Chinese Black Mushrooms: an edible fungus that grows on dead tree trunks. Soak in water until soft; cut off the stem before using.

⓯ Dried Wood Ears: an edible fungus that grows on dead tree trunks. Its shape resembled a human ear. Soak in water until soft before using. Large wood ears need to have the small hard stem removed before using.

⓰ Tiger Lily: Dried tiger lily bloom (pod). Soak in water until soft; remove the root (hard end).

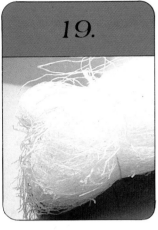

⑰ Dried Shredded Seaweed: Before using, rinse and soak in water for 1 hour. Change water several times during soaking. When it has expanded and become soft, it is ready for use.

⑱ Bean Thread Sheets: The bean thread sheets are made from mung beans. There are two kinds of bean thread skins, fresh and dried. Dried bean thread sheets must be blanched in water until soft before using.

⑲ Bean Threads: A type of thin, dried bean thread made from the mung bean. Soak in water until soft before using.

⑳ Bean Curd Sheets ("Bai Yeh"): (All bean curd products are made from soy beans.)

㉑ Bean Curd Stick ("Fu Dzu"): Deep-fry the bean curd stick until it expands; remove. Bring 3 c. water and 1/4 t. baking soda to a boil. Add bean curd stick; boil until soft. Remove and drain.

㉒ Bean Curd Skins ("Fu Pea"): Scald the bean curd milk; remove the skin and dry it.

㉓ Bean Curd: There are two kinds of bean curd, soft and hard.
Pressed Bean Curd: flattened to squeeze out the liquid. This bean curd may have a yellow, white, or brown outer surface. The color does not change the taste of the bean curd.

㉔ "Kau Fu": a spongy type of vegetarian ingredient made from wheat gluten. It is sliced and deep-fried to golden brown before using.

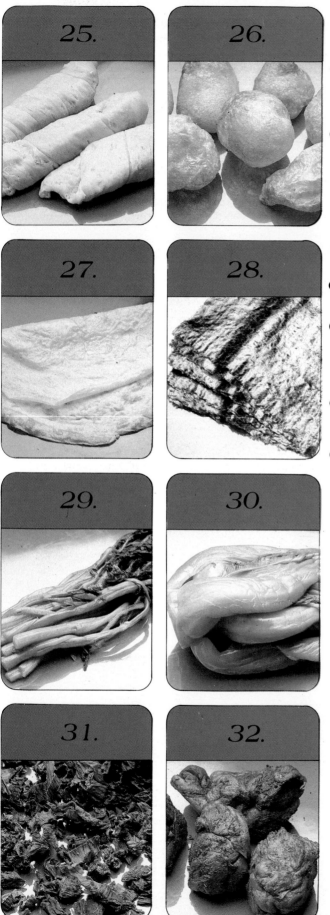

㉕ "Su Tsang": a type of long, thin roll made of wheat gluten. It is the main ingredient used in preparing vegetarian dishes.

㉖ Fried Gluten Balls ("Mien Chin Pao"): a type of light, round, deep fried ball made from wheat gluten and water, it must be cooked in water until soft; removed, and drained before using.

㉗ Egg Sheet: Heat the wok; lightly oil the lower two-thirds of the wok. Turn heat to low; add the beaten egg (s); swirl slowly to form a "pancake-like" sheet. When the egg is firm, carefully remove the egg sheet by lifting the edge. Turn it over and cook the other side; remove. The egg sheet will cook easily and hold better if a mixture of 1 Tbsp. of cornstarch and 1 Tbsp. of water is added to the beaten egg.

㉘ Nori: a combination of various algae pressed together to form a sheet. The sheet is then dried.

㉙ Salt Rape Greens ("Shueh Li Hone"): Rape greens marinated in salt.

㉚ Pickled Mustard Cabbage: There are two kinds of pickled mustard cabbage, sweet and salty. In this book, only salty pickled mustard cabbage is used. Salty pickled mustard cabbage is marinated in salt and allowed to ferment.

㉛ Dried Mustard Cabbage ("Mei Gan Tsai"): Cabbage that has been marinated in salt and then dried. Soak in warm water until soft; rinse before using.

㉜ Szechuan Pickled Mustard Greens: Marinated stems of mustard greens in salt, hot spices, and hot pepper powder. Before using, slice or shred the stems and soak them in water to remove the saltiness; remove and drain.

ARRANGEMENT OF SEATING ORDER AT A FEAST

The seat which faces the door is always regarded as the seat of honor and the seat which is near the door (i.e. facing the seat of honor) is for the host. The seating orders are designed to facilitate conversation among guests and the host. The various seating orders are illustrated and the seats marked as follows:

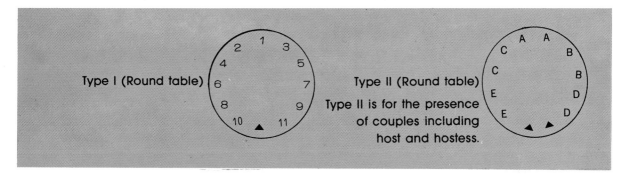

Type I (Round table)

Type II (Round table)

Type II is for the presence of couples including host and hostess.

ARRANGEMENT OF THE PLACE SETTING AT A FEAST

Chinese people pay much attention to the arrangement of the dinner place settings at a feast as they are directly related to the food and drinks. The cups, chopsticks, spoons, dishes and bowls, plates, wine pots, and tea cups are arranged according to a complete system. The arrangement of the place settings are shown in the following photos.

The arrangement of the dinner place sets for a table at a feast.

The arrangement of a place setting of each guest at a feast. The dinner place setting may be removed after it is used and replaced with a clean set as the feast progresses.

PRINCIPLES OF PLANNING MENUS

The vast region of China and the difference in geographical environment contribute to the wide variety of tastes and unique features of the food, drink, and snacks, Special attention should be given to the basic principles of arranging the menu for the family and the feast.

❶The various methods of cooking should not be repeated. For example, the many styles of cooking (i.e. stir-frying, deep-frying, steaming, stewing and braising, etc.) should be arranged to create a beautiful appearance, and prepared to stimulate the appetite.

❷The selection of ingredients should be harmonious without repetition. The major ingredients should include fish, meat (beef, pork, etc.) vegetables, fruit, bean and wheat products. When properly selected, they will accent each other and provide enjoyable eating.

❸The most important consideration is the harmony of the five tastes:sweet, salty, sour, bitter and spicy. Repetition should be avoided to provide a fresh and pleasing experience to the palate.

❹The complement of colors of the ingredients provide a pleasurable effect. Chinese food emphasizes a sense of beauty. Properly matched ingredients help to stimulate the appetite.

❺The dishes selected should be neither too easy nor to difficult to prepare. When serving, the food should be arranged alternately according to the complexity of preparation. All complicated dishes would be too time consuming to prepare, while all simple dishes would be too plain. The arrangement of the menu should allow the cook time to coordinate the work comfortably.

SAMPLE OF MENUS FOR BANQUETS AND FAMILY MEALS

In comparing Chinese and western-style cooking, the former is much more difficult to portion; therefore, it is necessary to follow a model to make sure each portion is sufficient for the number of guests. Today, most restaurants divide their serving dishes and bowls into three categories: large medium and small. Usually 8-10 large size serving dishes are adequate for a banquet meal of 10-12 guests. If there are 6 guests it is best to have about 5 medium size dishes. Below are suggested menus for banquets or family meals. (Dishes listed in menus are chosen from CHINESE CUISINE and CHINESE SNACKS by Huang Su-Huei.)

SAMPLES OF MENUS FOR BANQUETS (SERVES 12)

Example 1

Crispy Fried Cashews
Sliced Kidneys in Hot Sauce
Bon Bon Chicken
Jellyfish Salad

Braised Chicken with Shark's Fin
Saucy Crabs

Crispy-skin Chicken
Stuffed Egg Flower Soup
Stir-fried Crab Meat with Straw Mushrooms
Steamed Fish with Fermented Black Beans

"Four-flavor" Dumplings
Lotus Seed Soup

Example 2

Seven-star Appetizer Plate

Yellow Fish Soup
Stir-fried Shrimp with Green Peas
Crispy Pepper-skin Duckling
Three-flavored Soup

Braised Abalone with Assorted Vegetables
Sweet and Sour Fish

Meat, Shrimp, and Noodle Platter
Sweet Sesame Soup

Example 3

Variety Appetizer Platter
Stir-fried Squid with Dried Red Peppers
Stir-fried Chicken with Cashews

Shark' Fin Soup
Spicy Stir-fried Prawns
Bean Curd Rolls with Chopped Pork

Stewed Chicken with Chinese Black Mushrooms
Assorted Vegetable Platter
Fish Cooked in Soy Sauce

Eight-treasure Rice Pudding
Sweet Fruit Soup with White Wood Ears

A SAMPLE OF A MENU FOR A FAMILY MEAL

(SERVES 6)

Early preparation of certain materials allows you time to enjoy the company of your guests. Select materials that are readily available. Use simply utensils such as a wok and a cooking spoon to prepare delicious dishes. The sample menu includes five dishes and one soup and serves six. The following may be prepared beforehand.

❶ Cold Chicken Appetizer with Hot Sauce, see p. 33. Precook the chicken and cut it into pieces. Before serving, pour hot sauce over the chicken.

❷ Stir-fried Salty and Crispy Shrimp, see p. 111. Deep-fry shrimp; serve cold or deep-fry just before serving; serve hot.

❸ Beef with Nappa Cabbage in Oyster Sauce, see p. 91. Precook beef; cook the vegetable then line the platter. Stir-fry the beef with seasoning sauce then pour it over the vegetable before serving.

❹ Fish Slices in Tomato Sauce, see p. 107. Precook slices of fish and brown onion. Before serving, stir-fry all ingredients and tomato sauce together.

❺ Stir-fried Mushrooms and Chinese Broccoli, see p. 154. Prepare the stock. Add vegetables and cook just before serving.

❻ Mustard Greens and Pork Loin Soup, see p. 197. Prepare the stock and ingredients. Before serving, bring soup to a boil; add Szechuan mustard greens and green onions.

Lotus Blossom
Appetizer Platter

SERVES 12

(1) 24 slices of each:
  five-spice roast beef, see p 22
  "Chinese Cooking for Beginners"
  sliced ham, egg yolk cake (see below)
  roasted pork's ear (see below)
  tasty beef tongue, canned abalone

(2) 24 slices of each:
  tasty beef tongue, canned abalone, roasted
  Chinese black mushrooms.
  1 turnip, for flower garnish (colored red)
  2 cucumbers, thinly sliced
  1 tomato, sliced lengthwise
  1 carrot, shredded
  fresh coriander (cilantro) for garnish

● Trim each in (1) to the shape of a leaf. Arrange them as shown. Place a slice of material on one side of the middle slice; place a second slice on the opposite side. Continue arranging slices, alternating sides. Twelve slices complete the petal of the blossom. Carefully lift the completed "12 - leaf petal" and place it on one side of the platter. Continue to arrange 5 more ingredients; place them evenly around the platter. Six petals are used for the bottom layer. Arrange the second layer of petals as before. Place the second layer between petals of the first layer. Overlap the sliced cucumber and sliced tomato center of the platter. Place the shredded carrot in the center of the platter.

Garnish the platter with fresh coriander and flowers made from (2) . (Directions for garnish may be found in "Chinese Appetizers and Garnishes", p. 140)

To make egg-yolk cake; Mix 17 egg yolks with 1/2 tsp. salt, 2 Tbsp. each water and cornstarch into a rectangular or square mold. Steam for 20 minutes. To use; slice thinly.

To make roast pork's ear and black mushrooms; See p. 48 **To make tasty beef tongue;** See P. 62,

Fig. 1 Prepare the egg-yolks as directed.
Fig. 2 Pour the egg yolk mixture into a mold and steam for 20 minutes.

圓形拼盤　Variety Appetizer Platter

① 14 slices each:
　　cooked pork roast, cucumber
　　roasted black mushrooms
　　Beef shank, see p. 22, "Chinese
　　　Cooking for beginners"
　　Egg-yolk Cake, see p. 27
15 slices each: ham, canned abalone

② Ching Du Spareribs, see p. 69
Salt Water Shrimp, as many as
　desired, see p. 29
Jellyfish Salad, see p. 18, "Chinese
　Cooking for Beginners"

2 tomatoes
fresh parsley } for garnish

❶ Arrange the slices in ① by overlapping them around the platter in the order listed—pork roast to abalone.

❷ Cut the tomatoes in half lengthwise slice them. Arrange overlapping slices in a circle around the center of the platter.

❸ Place the Ching Du Spareribs on one side of the center of the platter then place the salt-water shrimps opposite the spareribs. Place the jellyfish salad in the middle on top of the shrimp and spareribs. For more details see "Chinese Appetizers and Garnishes", p. 139.

To prepare the roast pork: Preheat oven to 450°Cut 2 lbs. upper shoulder into long strips; add 1 1/2 T. cooking wine or sherry, 3 T, sugar, 2 t. salt, 1 1/2 T. Hoi Sin Sauce, mix and marinate for 6 hours. Place the meat in another pan and put it into the oven; Bake for 40 minutes at 400°-450°

■ **To roast black mushrooms:** (see p. 48 for marinade sauce) Cook black mushrooms in marinade sauce over medium heat until soft.

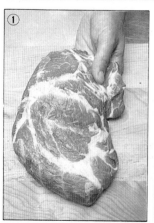

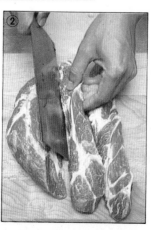

Fig.1　Use marbled upper shoulder pork roast

Fig.2　Cut the pork roast into long strips then marinate them.

柒星轉盤   Seven-Star Appetizer Plate   SERVES 12

① Bon Bon Chicken, see p. 35
    (portion as much as desired)
Five-color Rolls,
    (portions as much as desired)
12 slices Chicken in Aspic Slices,
    see p. 34
3 oz. Crispy Cashews, see "Chinese
    Cooking for Beginners", p. 19
Duck Gizzards
Kidneys in Hot Sauce, see p. 97
18 Salt Water Shrimps
lettuce, for garnish

● Place each ingredient in ① in separate serving bowls.
To make five-color rolls: Pare a turnip; place it in 1 c. water and 2 T. salt. Soak for 6 hours, or until soft. Remove and slice around the length of the turnip to obtain a 4-inch square piece. Place a slice of nori on the turnip square. Place a strip of chicken meat, ham, pickled cabbage, and cucumber at one end then roll it up. Cut the roll into 1-inch pieces. Continue cutting slices to obtain desired number of rolls. **To make duck gizzards:** Cut gizzards and remove any white membrane. Score the skin of the gizzards and drop them into a pot of boiling water. Remove them when cooked; the color changes.
To make salt water shrimp: Put 1 c. water, 1 T. cooking wine or sherry and 1 T. salt in a saucepan; bring to a boil. Place the shrimp in the saucepan, cook for 2 minutes; remove and drain.
To make dipping sauce for Duck Gizzards and Chicken in Aspic Slices: Mix 1 T. soy sauce; 1 T. white vinegar, and 1/2 T. shredded ginger root together. Or mix the hot chili paste with soy sauce.
To make dipping sauce for Salt Water Shrimp: Mix hot mustard with soy sauce.

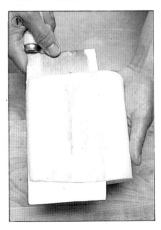

Fig.1 Five-color rolls:slice around the length of a white radish to obtain a 4-inch square piece.

Fig.2 Place a sheet of nori on the white radish square. Place a strip of chicken meat, ham, pickied cabbage, and cucumber at one end of a slice of nori then roll it up to form a baton-like shape.

三色拼盤　Three-ingredients Appetizer Platter

SERVES 6

4 oz. canned abalone (24 slices)
24 slices Beef Shark
   (see p. 22, "Chinese Cooking
   for Beginners")
3 oz. Jellyfish salad
   (see p. 18, "Chinese Cooking
   for Beginners")
1 cucumber

● Slice the cucumber and line the center of the platter. Arrange the slices of abalone and beef on the sides of the platter by slightly overlapping them. Place the jellyfish salad in the middle of the platter (on top of the abalone and beef slices.)

■ This appetizer is very simple to prepare. The ingredients may be purchased ready-made and substituted with other ingredients.

Fig.1　Abalone:Score the abalone 1/5 inch deep; do not cut through. Open the slits.

Fig.2　Turn the abalone so the cuts are horizontal then slice it.

雙色拼盤   **Two-ingredients Appetizers**   SERVES 6

24 slices roast pork (see p. 28)
1 4-oz. can abalone, cut into
   24 slices
2 cucumber

- Slice the cucumber and line the bottom of a platter. Arrange the slices of roast pork and abalone on two sides of the platter by slightly overlapping them. For more details of arrangement, see "Chinese Appetizers and Garnishes", p. 138.

Fig. 1 Cut the cucumber lengthwise in half. Slice across each half to 1/2 inch from the edge; cut through the 7th slice to form a set.

Fig. 2 Arrange the cucumber on the dish by fanning it slightly. Place the abalone and roast pork over the cucumber.

醉雞   **Drunken Chicken**

1 whole chicken or chicken legs
    (about 2 2/3 lbs.)

① { 1 green onion, cut into 6 pieces
    2 slices ginger root
    1 1/2 T. salt

② { 1 c. cooking wine or sherry
    1 c. chicken broth
    dash of salt

❶ Rub the exterior and the cavity of the chicken with ① ; leave ① in the cavity. Let stand for 3-4 hours. Remove the onion and ginger root from the cavity; rinse the chicken.

❷ Place the chicken in a large pot; pour water to cover half the chicken. Bring to a boil; cover and turn heat to low. continue to cook chicken for 15 minutes. Turn chicken over; cook for 10 more minutes. Remove chicken and allow to cool. Retain broth.

❸ Cut the chicken into bite-size pieces. Place the pieces of chicken, skin side down, in medium-size bowl. Add ② ; refrigerate for one day. To serve, put a plate over the bowl, tilt to drain liquid into a cup (retain liquid). Invert the bowl so that the chicken is in the center of the plate; remove the bowl. Pour the retained liquid on top of the chicken.

■ Chicken may be cut into four pieces, refrigerated then cut into smaller pieces when ready to serve.

Fig.1 Put a small plate over the bowl; tilt them to drain the liquid. Retain liquid.

Fig.2 Remove the small plate. Put the serving plate over the bowl and invert them so the chicken is in the center of the plate. Remove the bowl.

怪味雞　Cold Chicken Appetizers with Hot Sauce

SZECHUAN;
SERVES 6

① {
- 3 chicken legs (about 1 1/3 lbs.)
- 1 T. sesame paste or peanut butter
- 1 T. sugar
- 1 T. white vinegar
- 3 T. soy sauce
- 1 1/2 T. chopped green onions
- 1/2 T. ginger root, mashed or chopped finely
- 1/2 T. chopped garlic clove
- 2 T. hot pepper oil ("la you")
- 1 t. presoftened, chopped peppercorns

❶ Boil water in a large pot. Put the chicken in the water; water to cover half of the chicken. Cook for 15 minutes.Remove the chicken; retain broth for other uses. When the chicken is cool, cut it into bite-size pieces. Arrange on a serving plate.

❷ Separately place ingredients in ①, in order shown, in a bowl; mix after each addition. Pour mixture on top of the chicken and serve.

Fig.1 Cut each cooked chicken leg into 6 pieces.

Fig.2 Place 12 pieces of chicken on a plate then arrange the rest of the chicken on top of them.

雞肉凍   Chicken in Aspic

TAIWANESE;
SERVES 12

①
- 1 1/3 lbs. chicken legs
- 6 c. water
- 1 T. cooking wine or sherry
- 1 T. soy sauce
- 1/2 t. salt
- 1 green onion, cut into 4 pieces
- 2 thin slices ginger root

②
- 3 T. unflavored gelatin
- 1/2 c. water

❶ Blanch the chicken legs in a pot of boiling water. Remove the chicken legs and discard the water. Put the chicken legs and ① in a pot and cook over medium heat for 30 minutes. Remove the chicken legs; retain the broth. Tear the chicken into shreds; place the shredded chicken in a large mold. Add water in ② to gelatin; stir and let stand for 10 minutes.

❷ Continue to cook the retained broth until it boils down to 2 cups. Add the gelatin solution; continue to cook for 1 1/2 minutes. Strain the liquid to remove any ingredients; pour the liquid into the mold and refrigerate to set. Before serving, invert the mold on a platter and slice.

Dipping Sauce: 1 T. each soy sauce and white vinegar, 1/2 T. chopped ginger root.

Fig.1 Tear the chicken into shreds. Line a deep baking pan with the shredded chicken.

Fig.2 Pour the strained chicken broth over the shredded chicken.

棒棒鷄   **Bon Bon Chicken**

SZECHUAN;
SERVES 6

1/2 chicken or chicken legs
   (about 1 1/3 lbs.)
1 c. cooked bean thread sheets
   (cut into 1/4-inch strips)

① {
3 T. sesame paste or peanut butter
3 T. soy sauce
2 T. white vinegar
2 t. sugar
1 t. each: green onion
        ginger root } chopped
        garlic
1 T. hot pepper oil "la you"

❶ Place the chicken in a pot of boiling water, to cover. Cook for 15 minutes; remove. Allow to cool then tear into shreds. Place the bean thread strips in a pot of water and cook for 1 minute; do not overcook; remove vermicelli.

❷ Separately put ingredients ① in a bowl in order shown; mix after each addition (sauce).

❸ Arrange the strips of bean thread on a platter; then arrange the shredded chicken on top of the strips of bean threads. Pour the sauce over the chicken.

■ Finely shredded cucumber may line the platter before placing the strips of bean thread. If dried bean thread sheets are used, see P. 19, number 18.

Fig. 1   If dry sheets of bean thread are used, soak them in boiling water or hot water for 30 minutes.

Fig. 2   When the sheets of bean thread are soft, shred them then put them in a pot of boiling water. Cook for 1 minute; remove and serve.

35

葱油雞 Steamed Chicken with Green Onions

CANTONESE;
SERVES 12

① {
1 whole chicken (about 2 2/3 lbs.)

① {
1 T. salt
1 T. cooking wine or sherry
1 green onion, cut into 4 pieces
2 slices of ginger root
} combine

1/2 c. green onion
4 T. ginger root
} shredded
dash of black pepper

② {
1/2 T. cornstarch
1 T. water
} mix

❶ Wash the chicken and pat it dry. Rub the exterior and the cavity of the chicken with ① . Leave ① in the cavity of chicken; let stand for 1 hour. Place the chicken in a steamer, breast side up; steam over high heat for 25 minutes. Remove chicken; retain steaming liquid. Cut into bite-size pieces then put on a serving plate. Sprinkle the shredded green onion, shredded ginger root, and black pepper on the chicken.

❷ Heat 4 T. oil until smoking; drizzle over the chicken. Bring 1/2 c. of retained liquid to a boil; add mixture ② to thicken then pour it over the chicken.

Fig.1 Spread the shredded green onion and ginger root over the pieces of chicken.

Fig.2 Drizzle hot oil over the onions and ginger root to bring out the aroma and flavor.

油淋雞　　　　Shiny Chicken　　　　SERVES 6

<table>
<tr><td rowspan="8">①</td></tr>
</table>

1/2 chicken or chicken legs
　　(about 1 1/3 lbs.)
1/2 T. soy sauce
oil for frying

① {
1/4 c. green onions ⎫
1 T. ginger root　　⎬ chopped
1 1/2 T. sugar　　　⎭
2 T. white vinegar
2 1/2 T. soy sauce
1 t. sesame oil
}

❶ Wash the chicken and pat it dry. Rub soy sauce on the exterior and in the cavity of the chicken. Combine ① in a bowl.

❷ Heat the wok then add oil. Fry the chicken over high heat for 10 minutes, or until the skin is golden, crispy, and the meat is cooked. Remove the chicken; cut it into bite-size pieces. Place the pieces of chicken on a serving plate; pour mixture ① over the pieces of chicken.

■ Red hot peppers or minced garlic may be added to ① if desired.

■ If cooked chicken is being used, shorten the frying time. Remove the chicken when the skin is crispy.

Crispy Pepper-skin Chicken Legs

● See "Crispy Pepper-skin Duckling" (p. 56). Substitute duckling with chicken legs. Other ingredients are the same. Steam the chicken legs over high heat for 30 minutes.

紙包雞 Paper-wrapped Fried Chicken

SERVES 6

1/2 lb. chicken meat, cut into
    12 thin slices

① {
1/2 T. cooking wine or sherry
1/2 T. soy sauce
1/3 t. salt
1 t. sesame oil
dash of black pepper

12 Chinese pea pods
4 T. shredded green onion
2 T. shredded ginger root
12 5-inch square sheets cellophane
    paper
oil for frying

❶ Mix the chicken meat and ① in a bowl.

❷ *Place a slice of chicken on a sheet of cellophane paper. Place 1 Chinese pea pod, a portion of shredded green onion and shredded ginger root on top of the chicken. Wrap to form a rectangular packet. Repeat from *until all packets are formed.

❸ Heat the oil; fry the paper-wrapped chicken over high heat for 2 minutes. When the packets rise to the surface, use a slotted spoon to press them to the bottom of the wok to release any oil that is inside the packets. Remove the packets to a serving plate.

■ Shredded black mushrooms and shredded hot red pepper may be included in the paper-wrapped chicken.

Fig.1 After placing ingredients diagonally on the cellophane paper, fold the paper in half.

Fig.2 Roll the top edges of the cellophane paper toward the center to form the curry dumpling shape; twist the sides.

百花雞   **Stuffed Chicken Breasts**   TAIWANESE; SERVES 6

2/3 lb. boned chicken breasts or chicken legs

① {
1 T. cooking wine or sherry
1 T. cornstarch
1 egg white
2/3 t. salt
dash of black pepper
1/2 lb. raw, shelled shrimp
}

② {
water chestnuts
carrot
Chinese black mushrooms
green onions
} shredded to 1-inch lengths and combined to equal 1/2 cup

oil for frying

❶ Slit each piece of chicken lengthwise in half or in thirds to lie flat (butterfly); do not cut through. Mix ① together. Coat meat with half of mixture ①

❷ Clean and chop the shrimp finely. Add the remainder of mixture ① ; then add ② and mix. This will be the topping.

❸ Place the chicken on a flat surface, skin side down; sprinkle with cornstarch then evenly spread with the topping.

❹ Heat the wok then add oil. When the oil is hot, deep-fry the pieces of chicken over medium heat for 4 minutes, or until golden. Remove and drain. Slice the pieces into 1-inch widths and place on a serving plate. Dip into Szechuan peppercorn salt or ketchup before eating. (To prepare Szechuan peppercorn salt, see p. 17.)

Fig.1 Slit each piece of chicken lengthwise in half or thirds to lie flat (butterfly); do not cut through.

Fig.2 Place the chicken on a flat surface, skin side down; sprinkle with cornstarch then spread the topping evenly.

脆皮雞　　Crispy-Skin Chicken

CANTONESE;
SERVES 12

1 whole chicken (about 2 2/3 lbs.)

① { 1/4 t. five-spice powder
1 T. salt

② { 2 T. corn syrup or honey
1/2 c. hot water   } mix
1 T. white vinegar
1 T. cooking wine or sherry

oil for frying
dash of Szechuan peppercorn
salt (see. p. 16)

❶ Blanch the chicken in boiling water to remove any foreign matter; drain. Rub mixture ① on the exterior and in the cavity of the chicken. Use a toothpick to close the opening of cavity.

❷ Pour mixture ② over the chicken; baste chicken completely. Hang the chicken in a well-ventilated area to dry for about 7-8 hours.

❸ Heat the wok then add oil. Pierce the eyes of the chicken with a toothpick; this will prevent the eyes from popping during frying. Deep-fry the chicken over low heat for 20 minutes. Before removing, turn heat to high and cook until golden brown; remove and drain. Cut into bite-size pieces and arrange on a serving plate. Sprinkle lemon juice on top of the chicken and serve. Dip into Szechuan peppercorn salt before eating.

■ It is best to prepare this chicken dish on a sunny and breezy day to aid the drying process. The dryness of the skin will determine the crispiness.

■ If use oven, bake the chicken at 400° for 50 minutes.

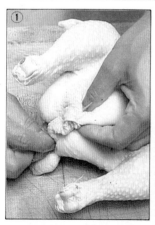

Fig.1 After rubbing mixture ① on the surface and in the cavity of the chicken, use a toothpick to close the opening of the cavity.

Fig.2 Baste the chicken several times with mixture ②

豆豉雞　　　Chicken with Black Beans

CANTONESE;
SERVES 6

1/2 chicken or 3 chicken legs
(about 1 1/3 lbs.)

① { 1/2 T. each: soy sauce, cooking
wine or sherry
1 T. cornstarch, 1/4 t. salt

oil for frying
1/4 chopped brown onion
1 1/2 T. fermented black beans
1/2 T. minced garlic clove

② { 1 T. soy sauce, 1/4 t. salt
dash of sesame oil
1/2 c. water, 1/2 T. cornstarch
1/2 bell pepper, diced } mix

❶ Cut the chicken into bite-size pieces; mix with ① and set aside for later use. Heat the wok then add oil; deep fry the chicken for 4 minutes, or until golden brown and the meat is cooked. Remove and drain. Remove the oil from the wok.

❷ Reheat the wok then add 3 T. oil. Sir-fry the brown onion until fragrant . Add fermented black beans and minced garlic; stir to mix. Add ② and chicken to wok; cook for 2 minutes, or until the sauce has thickened. Add bell pepper; stir to mix. Transfer to a serving dish and serve.

Country-style Fried Chicken

3 chicken lgs
oil

① { 1/2 T. each: cooking wine,
soy sauce
1/2 t. salt, 1 t. sugar

② { 1 egg yolk
2 T. cornstarch

③ { 1 T. each: onion, celery,
minced coriandeer
2 T. vinegar
1/4 t. Szechuan peppercorn

❶ Cut the chicken legs into bite-size pieces; mix with ① and set aside for later use. Add ② and mix before deep-frying.

❷ Heat the wok then add oil. Deep-fry the chicken for 4 minutes or until the skin is golden brown; remove and drain. Remove the oil from the wok.

❸ Reheat the wok then add 1 T. oil. Add the chicken and ③; stir to mix. Transfer to a serving dish and serve.

贵妃燒雞　　　**Royal Chicken**　　　CANTONESE;
SERVES 6

3 chicken legs (about 1 1/3 lbs.)
1/2 brown onion
1/2 c. carrot, cut into bite-size pieces

① {
2 T. each: soy sauce
　　　　cooking wine or sherry
3 T. Ketchup
1/4 t. salt
1 T. sugar
1/2 c. water
}

② {
1 t. cornstarch
1 T. water
} mix

❶ Wash the chicken legs and cut them into pieces. Cut the brown onion into bite-size pieces.
❷ Heat the wok then add 3 T. oil. Stir-fry the brown onion until fragrant. Add the pieces of chicken and stir to mix. Add the carrots and ① ; bring them to a boil. Turn the heat to low and cover; cook for 20 minutes, or until the liquid is reduced to 1/2 cup. Add mixture ② to thicken; stir. Transfer to a serving plate and serve.
■ When cooking the chicken, stir occasionally to prevent it from burning. If the liquid in the chicken mixture has not reduced to 1/2 cup after 20 minutes of cooking, turn the heat to high; stir and cook until the liquid is reduced to 1/2 cup.

Chicken with Chestnuts

3 chicken legs, cut into
pieces
1 T. soy sauce
oil
1/2 c. canned chestnuts

① {
1/2 T. sugar
1 T. cooking wine
3 T. soy sauce
dash of black pepper
1 c. water
}

② {
1 t. cornstarch
1 T. water
}
sesame oil
6 pieces green onion,
1 inch long

● Mix the chicken with soy sauce. Deep-fry the chicken until it is golden brown; remove and drain the cicken. Remove the oil from the wok. Cook the chicken and ① for 10 minutes or until the sauce is reduced to half. Add mixture ② to thicken; stir. Add the onions and sesame oil; serve.

家鄉屈雞   # Country-style Chicken

1 whole chicken (about 2 2/3 lbs.)
1 T. soy sauce, oil for frying
1 green onion, cut into 6 pieces
6 slices of ginger root

① { 1/2 c. dried tiger lily buds
1 c. dried wood ears
1/2 c. sliced bamboo shoots
3 Chinese black mushrooms

② { 5 T. soy sauce, 1 T. cooking wine or sherry
1 t. sugar, 5 c. water dash of black pepper

③ { 1 T. cornstarch
1 1/2 T. water } mix

❶ Wash the chicken and pat it dry. Rub the exterior and inside of cavity with soy sauce.
❷ Heat the wok then add oil. Deep-fry the chicken over high heat for 2 minutes, or until golden brown; remove and drain. Remove the oil from the wok. Put 2 T. oil in the wok; stir-fry the onion and ginger root until fragrant. Add ① and stir. Add the chicken and ② ; bring to a boil. Cover and let simmer for 10 minutes. Turn the chicken over and cook for another 10 minutes.
❸ Remove ① from the wok and place them on a serving platter. Cut the chicken into bite-size pieces and place them on the serving platter. Bring the remaining liquid to a boil; add mixture ③ to thicken; stir. Pour on top of the chicken. Garnish with sliced cucumber and tomato.

Three-cup Red-cooked Chicken

1/2 chicken
4 T. sesame oil
12 slices ginger root
3 dried hot red peppers

① { 1/4 c. each: cooking wine, soy sauce
1 T. sugar
1/2 c. water
1 c. soft bean threads, soak in water to soften

❶ Wash the chicken and cut it into pieces.
❷ Heat the wok then add the sesame oil. Stir-fry the ginger root and dried hot red pepper until fragrant. Add the chicken and stir-fry 3 minutes; remove to a deep pot. Add ①; simmer over low heat for 15 minutes. Add the bean threads; cook for 3 minutes or until the sauce has almost evaporated.

茄汁雞丁　Stir-fried Chicken in Tomato Sauce

SERVES 6

2/3 lbs. chicken meat
① { 1/2 T. cooking wine or sherry
　　 1 T. each: soy sauce, cornstarch
1/2 c. oil for frying
1 green onion, cut into 6 pieces
6 slices of ginger root
② { 1/4 c. each: black mushrooms, celery } diced
　　 1/2 c. each: bamboo shoots, carrot
　　 dash of salt
③ { 2 T. ketchup
　　 1/2 T. each: sugar, soy sauce
　　 3 T. water, 1/3 t. salt
　　 1 t. cornstarch, dash of black pepper

❶ Cut the chicken into 1/2-inch cubes. Add mixture①; mix thoroughly. Before frying, add 1 T. oil; mix so that the cubed meat will separate easily during frying. Mix③ in a bowl; set aside for later use.

❷ Heat the wok then add oil. Stir-fry the cubed chicken until cooked; remove (precooking). Remove the oil from the wok; reheat the wok and add 2 T. oil. Stir-fry onion and ginger root until fragrant. Add ② and 2 T. water; stir-fry until the liquid is reduced to almost dry and vegetables are cooked. Add chicken and ③. Turn the heat to high; stir to mix quickly then remove and serve.

■ Precooking ingredients in ② will shorten total cooking time.

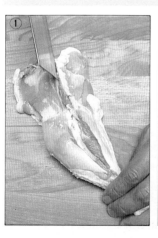 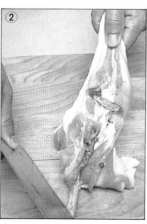

Fig.1 Cut down the middle of the chicken leg to the bone.

Fig.2 Break the joint and remove the bone. Cut the meat into 1-inch cubes (see page 45, Figs. 1 and 2).

宮保雞丁 Stir-fried Chicken with Dried Red Pepper

SZECHUAN;
SERVES 6

① {
2/3 lb. chicken meat
1/2 T. cooking wine or sherry
1 T. soy sauce
1 T. cornstarch
}

1/2 c. oil for frying
3 dried hot red peppers, diced
1 green onion, cut into 10 pieces

② {
1/2 T. cooking wine or sherry
2 T. each: soy sauce, water
2 t. sugar
1 1/2 t. each: cornstarch
white vinegar
}

1/3 c. fried cashews

❶ Use the blunt edge of a cleaver to lightly tenderize the chicken meat; cut the meat into 2/3-inch cubes. Add①; mix thoroughly. Before frying, add 1 T. oil and mix so that the cubed meant will sparate easily during frying.

❷ Heat the wok then add oil. Stir-fry the chicken meat until cooked; remove (precooking). Remove the oil from the wok. Reheat the wok then add 1 T. oil. Use low heat to stir-fry the diced hot red peppers until fragrant. Add chicken, onions, and ②. Turn heat to high and quickly stir-fry. Add cashews; mix.

■ To prepare Fried Cashews, see p. 19, "Chinese Cooking for Beginners". Roasted cashews may be used.

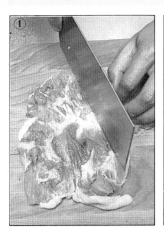

Fig.1 Boning a chicken leg (see p. 44). Score the meat lightly so that the meat will be tender after frying.

Fig.2 Cut the meat into strips then cut it into 2/3-inch cubes.

腰果雞丁　Stir-fried Chicken with Cashews

CANTONESE;
SERVES 6

2/3 lb. chicken meat

① { 1/3 t. salt
1/2 T. cooking wine or sherry
1 T. each: cornstarch, water

1/2 c. oil for frying
1 green onion, cut into 6 pieces
1/2 c. diced cucumber

② { 1/2 t. each: salt, sugar
dash of black pepper
dash of sesame oil
2 T. water
1 t. cornstarch
2/3 c. fried cashews

❶ Tenderize the chicken meat with a meat mallet; cut it into 1/2 inch cubes. Add ① and mix. Before stir-frying, add 1 T. oil and mix so that the cubed meat will separate easily during frying. Place ② in a bowl and mix; set aside for later use.

❷ Heat the wok then add oil. Stir-fry chicken meat until cooked; remove (precooking). Remove the oil from the wok. Reheat the wok then add 1 T. oil. Stir-fry onions until fragrant. Add cucumber; stir-fry for 1 minute. Add chicken meat and ②. Turn heat to high and quickly stir-fry. Add fried cashews and mix; remove and serve.

■ To prepare Fried Cashews, see p 19, "Chinese Cooking for Beginners". Roasted cashews may be used.

■ Boning chicken legs see pages 44 and 45, Figs. 1 and 2. Stir-fry chicken See P. 47, Figs. 1, 2 and 3.

Stir-fried Chicken with Walnuts

● See ingredients and directions for "Stir-fried Chicken with Cashews"; substitute walnuts for cashews. Green pepper, onion, carrot, bamboo shoot, etc. may be added to taste.

辣子雞丁 Spicy Chicken with Water Chestnuts

SZECHUAN;
SERVES 6

① 2/3 lb. chicken meat
  { 1/2 T. cooking wine or sherry
  1 T. each: cornstarch, soy sauce
  1/2 c. oil for frying
② { 1 T. each: (chopped)
    green onion, ginger root, garlic clove
    1/2 T. hot chili paste
  8 water chestnuts
③ { 1/2 T. cooking wine or sherry, 1 T. soy sauce
    1 1/2 T. water, 2 t. sugar
    1 t. each: cornstarch, white vinegar
    dash of sesame oil
    dash of Szechuan peppercorn powder

❶ Cut the chicken meat into 1/2-inch cubes. Add ① and mix; marinate for 20 minutes. Before stir-frying, add 1 T. oil and mix so that the cubed meat will separate easily during frying. Dice the water chestnuts. Place ③ in a bowl; mix and set aside for later use.

❷ Heat wok then add oil. Stir-fry the chicken meat until cooked; remove and drain (precooking). Remove the oil from wok. Reheat the wok then add 2 T. oil. Add ②; stir-fry until fragrant. Add water chestnuts and stir-fry to mix; add chicken meat and ③. Turn heat to high; quickly stir-fry to mix. Remove and serve.

■ Szechuan peppercorn powder may be omitted.
■ Boning chicken legs (See pages 44 and 45, Figs. 1 and 2).

Fig. 1, 2 Heat the wok then add oil. Stir-fry the chicken.

Fig. 3 Stir-fry the chicken until it is cooked; it will turn white. Remove and drain.

桶子油雞　　Roasting Chicken in Soy Sauce

CANTONESE;
SERVES 12

① {
1 whole chicken or chicken legs (about 2 2/3 lbs.)
6 c. water
6 T. cooking wine or sherry, or Shoahsing wine
1/2 T. salt
4 oz. rock sugar or granulated sugar
}

② {
Szechuan peppercorns
Star anise
dried orange peel
stick cinnamon
whole cloves
fennel
licorice powder
} combined to equal 1/2 oz.

3 c. soy sauce

- Place ① and ② in a pot. Add 3 c. soy sauce. Cook over low heat for 20 minutes (braising sauce). Place the chicken in the sauce; spoon braising sauce over the chicken and inside the cavity of the chicken. Cover and simmer for 10 minutes. Turn the chicken over and cook for 10 more minutes. Turn off heat and let stand for 20 minutes. Remove the chicken from the sauce and let cool. Brush the surface of the chicken with sesame oil; cut into large bite-size pieces; place on a serving plate. Pour some braising sauce over the chicken;　serve.
- ■ Ingredients ② may be purchased at many Chinese herbal stores.
- ■ The braising sauce may be used to cook liver, pork tongue, hard boiled eggs, seaweed, and pressed bean curd. To keep sauce from spoiling, if kept for a long time, boil the sauce every 3 days, cool, then refrigerate until next use.

Roasted Pigs' Ears

3 pigs' ears
braising sauce
green onion or coriander

shredded ginger root
sesame oil

- Cook the pigs' ears in water for 30 minutes. Transfer the ears to the braising sauce; cook for 20 minutes. Turn off the heat; soak the ears for 10 minutes. Remove and allow to cool. Slice the pigs' ears then arrange them on a serving plate. Place coriander and shredded ginger root on the edge of the plate; sprinkle with sesame oil.

48

金華玉樹雞 Grilled Ham and Chicken Slices

CANTONESE;
SERVES 12

1 whole chicken (about 2 2/3 lbs.)

① {
1 T. salt
1 T. cooking wine or sherry
1 green onion, cut into 6 pieces
2 slice ginger root
}

20 slices of ham (about 4 oz.)

② {
1 t. cornstarch
2 t. water
} mix

broccoli for garnish

❶ Rub the exterior and the cavity of the chicken with ① and let stand for 1 hour. Place the chicken, breast side up, on a heat-proof platter. Steam, over high heat, for 20 minutes. Remove the chicken; retain the broth. Allow the chicken to cool then bone. Cut the chicken meat into pieces 2 inches wide and 1 inch thick.

❷ Arrange the ham and pieces of chicken alternately on a serving plate.

❸ Bring 1 cup chicken broth to a boil; salt to taste. Thicken broth with mixture ② ; stir. Pour the thickening on top of the chicken. Arrange the brocoli around the serving platter.

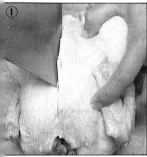

Fig.1 Make a cut on the breast and back.

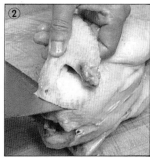

Fig.2 Make a cut at the base of the wings.

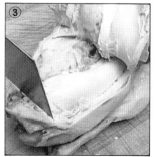

Fig.3 Pull the meat down and away from the bones.

49

蠔油扒雞翼 Chicken Wings with Oyster Sauce

CANTONESE;
SERVES 6

12 chicken wings (about 1 lbs.)
1 T. soy sauce
 oil for frying
1 green onion, cut into 6 pieces
6 slices ginger root

① {
2 T. oyster sauce
1/4 t. salt
1 t. sugar
dash of black pepper
1 c. water
}

② {
1/2 T. cornstarch
1 T. water
} mix

❶Clean the chicken wings; pat them dry. Add 1 T. soy sauce and mix them together.
❷Heat wok then add oil. Deep-fry wings until golden brown; remove. Remove the oil from the wok. Reheat the wok then add 2 T. oil. Stir-fry the onions and ginger root until fragrant. Add chicken wings and ① ; cover and cook for about 5 minutes, or until liquid is reduced to 1/2 cup. Thicken with mixture ② ; stir.
■Precooked vegetables may line the bottom of the serving plate before placing the chicken wings on platter.

Chicken Wings with Sauce

12 chicken wings
(about 1 1/3 lbs.)
1 c. shredded onion
1 c. tomato, diced coursely

① {
1 T. each: cooking wine, vinegar, soy sauce
1 1/2 T. each: lemon juice, sugar
1/2 t. salt, 1 dried hot pepper
1 c. water, 1/2 T. sesame oil
}

3 T. oil

② {
1/2 T. cornstarch
1 T. water
} mix

❶ Deep-fry the chicken wings until golden brown (see steps 1 and 2 of "Chicken Wings with Oyster Sauce").
❷ Heat the wok then add 3 T. oil. Stir-fry the onions and tomato. Add ① and chicken wings. Simmer over low heat for 10 minutes until the sauce is reduced to half. Add mixture ② and stir; remove and serve.

杏花酥雞翼   Stuffed Chicken Wings

① 12 chicken wings
dash of cooking wine or sherry
dash of salt
1 T. cornstarch

2/3 lb. shelled shrimp
1/2 oz. pork fat
② 1 t. cooking wine or sherry
1/2 t. salt
1 egg white
1 T. cornstarch
1 T. chopped roasted almonds
or roasted peanuts
oil for frying

❶ Cut off the tips of the chicken wings. Cut the skin on the top side of the wing and remove the bone through the thick end. Add ① and mix with the chicken wings.

❷ Clean the shrimp and pat them dry. Finely chop the pork fat and shrimp together. Add ② and mix thoroughly (filling). Divide the filling into 12 portions.

❸ Open the cicken wing to lie flat; place one portion of filling on the wing. Dip a spoon in water (to prevent filling from sticking); remove and smooth the surface of the filling.(See P. 152, Figs. 1, 2) Sprinkle the filling with chopped almonds.

❹ Heat the wok then add oil. Deep-fry the stuffed chicken wings over medium heat for 5 minutes, or until golden brown; remove and serve.

Fig.1 Make a cut down the middle of the chicken wings.

Fig.2 Remove the bone by starting at the joint.

炸雞腰窩渣　　**Chicken Kidney Fritters**　　

4 oz. chicken kidneys
① { 2 1/2 c. chicken stock
1/2 T. cooking wine or sherry
3/4 t. salt

② { 5 T. water
3 egg yolks } mix
1/2 c. cornstarch

1 c. cornstarch
oil for frying

❶ Lightly score the membrane of the kidneys and squeeze them to remove the kidney meat; place in a pot. Add ① and bring to a boil. Slowly add ② while stirring. Cook and stir for about 2-3 minutes. Add 1 T. oil; mix thoroughly. Pour the mixture on an oiled plate; refrigerate to set. When set and cool, cut into 2-inch diamond-shaped pieces.

❷ Dip the diamond-shaped pieces in water then coat them with cornstarch.

❸ Heat the wok then add oil; deep-fry the kidney pieces over high heat for 4 minutes, or until golden. Remove and serve.

■ The pieces of kidney must be deep-fried in several batches to maintain the high heat of the oil and to prevent them from becoming soft.

■ Pork brain may be used as a substitute; however, first remove the menbrane with a toothpick and rinse. Steam with 1 green onion, 1 slice ginger root, and ½ T. cooking wine for 5 minutes over medium heat. Follow cooking procedures given above.

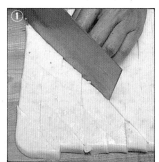

Fig.1 When the cooked kidney mixture is cool and set, cut it diagonally into diamond-shaped pieces.

Fig.2 Use a strainer to place the kidney pieces in the wok. Deep-fry in batches. of 5 to 8 pieces.

Fig.3 Deep-fry until golden brown; remove.

炒鴿鬆　　Fried Minced Squab

CANTONESE;
SERVES 12

① {
1 squab (about 2/3 lb.)
1/2 lb. pork tenderloin
3 chicken livers, 1 oz. chicken fat
dash of black pepper
1 egg yolk
}
2 chopped Chinese black mushrooms
1/2 c. each: (chopped) brown onion,
　　　　　　bamboo shoot, celery

② {
2 T. water, 1 T. soy sauce
1/2 t. each: salt, sugar
1 t. cornstarch
dash of sesame oil
}
1/4 c. precooked green peas
1 oz. fried rice noodles
24 leaves iceberg lettuce

❶ Bone the squab. Mince the squab, pork, livers, and chicken fat. Add ① and mix together.
❷ Heat wok then add 2 T. oil. Stir-fry the meat mixture until all the liquid has evaporated. Move mixture aside; add onion, Chinese black mushrooms; stir-fry until fragrant. Add bamboo shoots and celery;stir to mix. Return the meat to the center of the wok; stir-fry with other ingredients over high heat. Add ② and green peas; mix then remove.
❸ Place the fried noodles on a plate; spoon the minced squab on top of the rice noodles. Lettuce leaves are used to wrap around the meat and noodle mixture.
To prepare fried rice noodles: Heat the wok then add oil.Heat the oil until it is very hot. Turn off the heat, add dried rice noodles. When the noodles rise to the surface,turn them over. Fry the noodles until both sides are light golden; remove.
■ If squab is not used, increase the amount of pork loin to 2/3 lbs.

Deep-fried Squabs

4 squabs
2 T. soy sauce
oil
1/2 c. onion

① {
1 1/2 T. each: sugar, cooking
　　　　　　　wine, sesame oil
2 T. each: lemon juice, ket-
　　　　　chup, hot pepper paste
1 t. salt, 1 1/2 c. water
}

❶ Clean the squabs then cut off the legs. Brush them with soy sauce and deep-fry until golden brown.
❷ Heat the wok then add 3 T. oil. Stir-fry the onions; and ① and the squabs. Cook for 8 minutes or until the sauce is reduced to 1/2 cup. Remove the squabs and cut them into quarters. Place the squabs on a serving plate; pour the sauce over the squabs.

53

芋泥鴨 Fried Duckling with Taro Stuffing

1 duckling (about 3 1/3 lbs.)

① {
2 T. soy sauce
1 T. salt, 1 green onion, 2 slices ginger root, dash of cooking wine or sherry
1 t. Szechuan peppercorns, 1 star anise
}

1 1/2 c. precooked taro root

② {
1/2 t. each: salt, sugar, sesame oil
dash of five-spice powder
1 T. lard, 1 1/2 T. cornstarch
1/4 c. chopped fresh coriander (cilantro)
}

③ {
1 egg
1 T. cornstarch
}

oil for frying

④ {
1/2 c. duckling broth
1 T. each: chopped green onion, ginger root
1 t. cornstarch
}

❶ Rub the exterior and cavity of the duckling with ①. Steam it over high heat for 2 hours, or until soft. Remove; retain the broth. Bone the duckling and place it, skin side down, on the working surface. Cut off the thick part of the meat then trim to flatten it. Dice the meat that was removed. Rub ③ on top of the square piece of meat.

❷ Mix the taro root and ② together with the diced meat; place this mixture on top of the square piece of meat. (Combined thickness should be 1 inch). Sprinkle with cornstarch; cut into 2-inch strips.

❸ Heat the wok then add oil. Deep-fry the strips of stuffed meat over medium heat for 8 minutes, or until golden brown. Remove and cut into bite-size pieces. Place on a serving plate. Bring ④ to a boil (dipping sauce); serve.

Fig.1 Peel and slice the taro root. Steam it until soft. Remove and mash it with the flat side of a cleaver or use an electric beater.

Fig.2 Add ② and the diced meat to the mashed taro root; mix well then place on top of the piece of meat.

樟茶鴨 Crispy Smoked Duckling

SZECHUAN;
SERVES 12

1 duckling (about 3 1/3 lbs.)

①
- 1 1/2 T. salt
- 1 t. Szechuan peppercorn
- 1 star anise, 1 t. saltpeter or niter

②
- 1/4 c. hickory chips
- 2 T. tea leaves
  } or
- 1/4 c. tea leaves
- 2 T. sugar

oil for frying

24 pieces of green onion, approximately 2 inches long

③
- 2 T. sweet bean paste
- 2 T. each: sugar, water

❶ Stir-fry ① over low heat until the salt is light brown. Rub ① on the exterior and in the cavity of the duckling. Let stand for 2-6 hours rinse then steam it over high heat for 40 minutes.

❷ Preheat the oven to 450°. Place the duckling in the middle rack of the oven. Place ② on a tray and put it on the bottom rack of the oven. Bake the duckling for 5 minutes, or until the skin becomes golden brown. Remove.

❸ Heat the wok then add oil. Deep-fry the smoked duckling over medium heat for 8 minutes, or until the skin becomes crispy; remove. Cut the duckling into bite-size pieces and place on a serving plate.

❹ Reheat the wok then add 4 T. sesame oil; add ③ ; stir-fry to mix. (This is the dipping sauce for the duckling.) Serve with green onion.

Steamed Duckling with Sour Plums

1 duckling
2 T. soy sauce
oil

②
- 1/2 T. cornstarch
- 1 T. water
  } mix

①
- 2 slices each: green onion, ginger root
- 1 T. each: diced garlic, soy sauce cooking wine
- 2 T. hot bean paste
- 3 T. rock candy or sugar
- 1/4 c. sour plums, remove pits
- 1 t. salt

❶ Rub the surface of the duckling with soy sauce then deep-fry it until golden brown; remove.

❷ Heat the wok then add 2 T. oil. Add ① and cook it until the rock candy has dissolved. Place the mixture in the cavity of the duckling. Steam the duckling for 2 hours or until the meat is soft; remove and cut it into pieces. Arrange the pieces of duckling on a serving plate. Add mixture ② to the sauce; stir. Pour the sauce on the pieces of duckling.

香酥鴨   **Crispy Pepper-skin Duckling**

1 duckling (about 3 1/3 lbs.)

① {
3 green onions
4 slices of ginger root
2 T. cooking wine or sherry
1 1/2 T. salt
1 t. Szechuan peppercorns
1 star anise
}

1 T. soy sauce
oil for frying
dash of Szechuan peppercorn salt

❶ Combine ① and rub the mixture on the surface and in the cavity of the duckling. Marinate for 30 minutes. Steam the duckling over high heat for 2 hours, or until soft; remove. While the duckling is still hot, rub it with 1 T. soy sauce.

❷ Heat the wok then add oil. Deep-fry the duckling for 10 minutes, or until golden brown. Remove and cut it into bite-size pieces; place them on a serving plate. Dip into Szechuan peppercorn salt before eating.

■ Quartered pieces of toast or dumplings may be arranged around the platter.

■ To prepare Szechuan Peppercorn Salt, see p. 17.

Fig.1 Cut off the webs and wing tips of the duckling. Rub the duckling with ①. Steam until soft. Rub the duckling with soy sauce while it is still hot.

Fig.2 Place the duckling in a large strainer to hold it together while deep-frying it. Put the duckling in the oil and deep-fry it.

八珍抓鴨　Eight-treasure Braised Duckling

CANTONESE;
SERVES 12

1 duckling (about 3 1/3 lbs.)
1 T. soy sauce
oil for frying

① {
1 green onion, cut into 6 pieces
2 slices ginger root, 5 T. soy sauce
1 T. sugar, 2 T. cooking wine or sherry
5 C. water, 1 star anise, dash of Szechuan peppercorns
}

② {
2 sea cucumbers (see p. 18)
1/4 c. button mushrooms, 1 pork kidney
1 duck gizzard, 1 duck liver
3 Chinese black mushrooms
6 slices each: bamboo shoots, carrot, cucumber
}

③ {
1 1/2 T. cornstarch
2 T. water
} mix
dash of sesame oil

❶ Make a deep vertical cut down the back of duckling; rub exterior and cavity with soy sauce. Heat wok then add oil. Deep-fry duckling for about 2 minutes, or until golden brown; transfer duckling to a deep pot. Add①; bring to a boil. Cover; cook over low heat for 1 1/2 hours, or until the meat is tender and liquid has reduced to 2 cups.

❷ Cut sea cucumbers to bite-size pieces. Cut pork kidney in half; remove any white membrane. Score lengthwise and crosswise; cut to bite-size pieces. Cut gizzard and liver in same manner. Separately, cook sea cucumbers, pork kidney, gizzard, liver, bamboo shoot, and carrot in boiling water.

❸ Place the duckling on a serving plate; bring the duckling broth to a boil. Add②; boil. Add mixture③ to thicken; stir. Sprinkle in sesame oil then pour over the duckling.

■ Amount in② could be increased or decreased. Fish skin, shark's fin, squid, roast pork, scallops, and Chinese cabbage may be added.

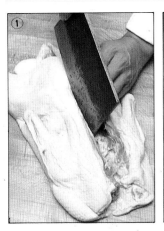

Fig.1 Make a deep vertical cut down the center of the duckling.
Fig.2 Remove the back bone before cooking.

銀芽拌鴨絲　Roasted Duckling Salad

① {
1/4 pre-roasted duckling,
　　shredded by hand
1/2 c. salted jellyfish, shredded
1/4 c. precooked shredded
　　bell pepper
1 c. precooked bean sprouts
1 egg sheet, shredded
}

② {
2 T. sesame paste or peanut butter
2 T. white vinegar
2 T. each: ketchup, water
1 T. soy sauce
1/2 T. sugar
1/2 t. salt
dash of sesame oil
}

● Separately place ② in a bowl in order listed; mix after each addition. Mix ① into mixture ② ; place on a serving plate and serve.

■ Pre-roasted duckling may be purchased at some markets.

■ To prepare the jellyfish:
Shred the jellyfish and plunge it into boiling Water; stir quickly. Remove the jellyfish then plunge it into cold water; rinse several times. Soak the jellyfish in cold water for 4 or 5 hours until it expands and returns to its original Shape. Remove and drain.

■ To make egg sheet, see P. 79, Figs. 1, 2, 3.

Ham and Bean Thread Salad

① {
1 c. shredded ham
2 c. bean threads, soaked, cooked
　　and cut
1 c. peeled, shredded cucumber
3 T. coriander
}

② {
4 T. mayonnaise
1 T. sesame oil
1/3 t. salt
}

● Place ① and ② in a bowl and mix. Chill before serving.

鳳梨炒肫球 Stir-fried Sweet and Sour Duck Gizzards
CANTONESE; SERVES 6

6 duck gizzards
1 T. cooking wine or sherry
1 bell pepper ⎤ cut into bite-size
2/3 c. pineapple ⎦ pieces

① {
1 green onion, cut into 6 pieces
6 slices of ginger root
1 hot red pepper, cut into small pieces
}

② {
2 T. each: sugar, water
1 1/2 T. each: ketchup, white vinegar
2/3 t. each: salt, sesame oil
1 t. cornstarch
}

❶ Cut each gizzard into quarters; remove the membrane. Lightly cut each piece lengthwise and crosswise; do not cut through. Mix with wine; marinate for 5-10 minutes. Put in a pot of boiling water; cook until color changes. Remove. Add 1/2 t. salt to pineapple; let stand for 20 minutes. Drain the water from the pineapple.

❷ Heat wok then add 3 T. oil; stir-fry ① until fragrant. Add pineapple; stir to mix. Add②; bring to a boil. Add gizzards and bell pepper; stir to mix thoroughly. Place on serving plate; serve.

■ If chicken gizzards are used; cut each gizzard in half.

  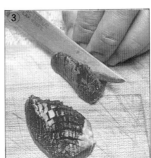

Fig.1, 2 Cut away the membrane of the gizzards.

Fig.3 Make vertical and horizontal cuts on the inside surface of the gizzards; do not cut through

燒焗鳳肝   Sweet and Sour Chicken Livers

CANTONESE;
SERVES 6

① {
1 lb. chicken livers
1 T. cooking wine or sherry
1/3 t. salt

② {
2 1/2 T. ketchup
1/2 T. soy sauce
1/2 T. white vinegar
3/4 T. sugar
5 T. water
oil for frying
1 T. sesame oil

❶ Wash and clean the chicken livers; drain the water and cut the livers into bite-size pieces. Lightly cut the livers lengthwise and crosswise; do not cut through. Add①; mix with chicken livers. Marinate for 5-10 minutes. Place ② in a bowl; mix thoroughly then set aside for later use.

❷ Heat wok then add oil; deep-fry the chicken livers for about 4 minutes, or until golden brown. Remove.

❸ Heat wok then add 1 t. sesame oil; add chicken livers and ②. Turn heat to high and cook for 2-3 minutes, or until the liquid has almost evaporated; remove and serve.

■ Serve this dish hot or cold. This is a good dish to serve with wine.

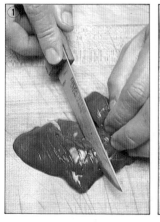 

Fig.1 Lightly cut the livers lengthwise and crosswise; do not cut through.

Fig.2 Cut the livers into pieces.

醬肉   **Saucy Ham**

2 2/3 lbs. fresh ham

① {
4 T. sweet bean paste
2 T. each: cooking wine or sherry,
            sugar
8 T. soy sauce

② {
6 c. water
1/4 t. five-spice powder
1 green onion, cut into 4 pieces
2 slices ginger root

❶ Clean the fresh ham. Mix ① in order shown. Add mixture ①, ② and the ham in a deep pot. Cook over low heat for about 2 hours, or until meat is cooked and the liquid has reduced to 1/2 cup. If there is too much liquid turn the heat to high and cook longer until liquid reduces to 1/2 cup. Remove the ham; retain liquid.

❷ After the ham is cool, cut it into thin slices. Arrange the slices on a serving plate. Pour the retained liquid on top of the ham.

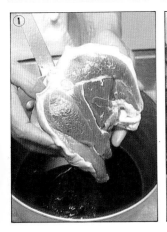

Fig.1 After mixing ingredients ① and ②, as listed, in a pot, add the ham.

Fig.2 Cook over low heat until the ham is cooked and the sauce is reduced to 1/2 cup.

肴肉　　　Tasty Chinese ham Slices　　SERVES 12

2 2/3 lbs. fresh ham
1 t. niter or saltpeter

① 2 T. salt
1 t. Szechuan peppercorns

② 2 green onions
2 slices ginger root
1 T. cooking wine or sherry
8 c. water

③ 1/2 T. each: soy sauce, white vinegar
1 t. sugar
1 t. each: chopped ginger root,
chopped green onion

❶ Clean the ham then pat it dry. Rub the ham with niter. Stir-fry ①
until the salt is golden; remove and rub it into the surface of the
ham. Marinate for 3 days.

❷ Rinse the ham lightly; place it in a pot and add ② ; cook for 1
hour over low heat, or until the meat is cooked. Remove when
cooked and wrap it tightly with a dish towel. Place a heavy
weight on top of the ham to compress it. Let cool. Unwrap the
ham and cut it into slices. Arrange the slices on a serving
plate. Place 3 in a bowl and mix; serve with sliced ham as
dipping sauce.

■ Ham will keep in refrigerator for 3-4 days after cooking.

■ Niter is an ingredient that aids in preservation; if unavailable,
omit.

Tasty Beef Tongue

● Ingredients and directions are the same as for "Tasty Chinese Ham
Slices" except substitute beef tongue for the ham.

紅燒肉   **Cubed Pork in Soy Sauce**   TAIWANESE; SERVES 6

1 lb. bacon slab
4 garlic cloves, mashed

① { 3 T. cooking wine or sherry
4 T. soy sauce
5 T. wate

3 green onions, cut into
    1-inch pieces

● Cut the bacon into 1 1/2-inch pieces; place them in a pot. Add garlic and ① ; cover and cook over low heat for 30 minutes. When cooked, stir occasionally to prevent buring. When the liquid has almost complelety evaporated , sprinkle in the pieces of green onion. Remove to a serving plate.

■ A dash of sugar may be added if a sweet taste is desired.
■ The whole slab of bacon may be cooked first then cut. The pieces of bacon will retain their shape better by using this method.

Cubed Pork with Bamboo Shoots

1 lb. bacon slab, cut into
    pieces
6 pieces green onion, 1-inch
    long
4 garlic cloves, mashed
1 1/2 c. cubed bamboo
      shoots
2 T. oil

① { 1 T. cooking wine
5 T. soy sauce
1/2 T. sugar
1 1/2 c. water

● Heat the wok then add 2 T. oil. Stir-fry the bacon until golden brown. Add the onions, garlic, bamboo shoots, and ①. Cover and cook over low heat for 40 minutes or until the sauce is reduced to 1/2 cup.

回鍋肉　Double-cooked Pork Slices

SZECHUAN;
SERVES 6

① {
1/2 lb. precooked ham
2/3 c. sliced, pressed bean curd
4 oz. or 1/4 cabbage
1 fresh garlic
1/2 T. cooking wine or sherry
1 t. hot bean paste
1 T. sweet bean paste
1 T. soy sauce
dash of sugar
}

❶ Slice the precooked ham. Cut the cabbage into bite-size pieces. Diagonally cut the fresh garlic into small pieces; separate the white and green pieces. Mix ① together in a bowl and set aside for later use.

❷ Heat the wok then add 2 T. oil. Stir-fry the cabbage and 1 T. water over high heat until the cabbage is soft; remove.

❸ Reheat the wok then add 2 T. oil. Stir-fry the ham. Add the pressed bean curd; stir-fry to mix. Remove. Add the white pieces of garlic, stir-fry until fragrant. Add ① and bring to a boil. Add ham and pressed bean curd; stir to mix. Add cabbage; stir to mix. Sprinkle in the green pieces of garlic; remove and serve.

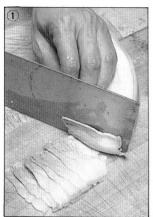 

Fig.1　Slice the cooked ham.

Fig.2　Slice the pressed bean curd.

蒜泥白肉　Pork Slices with Chopped Garlic

SZECHUÁN;
SERVES 6

① 1 lb. fresh ham (fatty)

① { 1 T. cooking wine or sherry
1 green onion
2 slices ginger root

6 garlic cloves

② { 3 T. soy sauce
1 1/2 t. each: sugar, white vinegar
1 1/2 T. hot pepper oil

❶ Clean the ham and place it in a deep pot. Add water to cover; add ①. Cover and bring to a boil. Turn the heat to low and cook for 30 minutes. Remove the ham and cut it into paper-thin slices. Before serving, blanch the slices of ham in boiling water then arrange them on a serving plate.

❷ Mash the garlic and put it in a bowl; add ② and mix. Pour this mixture over the ham slices. Serve.

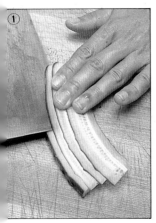
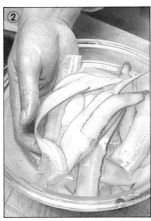

Fig.1 Cut the cucumber lengthwise into thin slices.

Fig.2 Soak the cucumber in cold water for 10 minutes. Remove and put on a plate. Serve with "Pork Slices with Chopped Garlic".

梅菜扣肉　　Steamed Pork with "Mei Gan Tsai"

SERVES 12

1 lb. fresh bacon (about 3 inches thick)

5 T. soy sauce

2 c. oil for frying

2 c. dried mustard cabbage ("Mei Gan Tsai")

1 green onion, cut into 6 pieces

6 slices ginger root

① { 1 T. cooking wine or sherry
2/3 T. sugar
1/2 c. retained broth (from bacon)

❶ Place the bacon in a pot; add water to cover. Cook over low heat for about 30 minutes. Remove the bacon. Retain broth(add to ①). Lightly pierce the skin of the bacon to prevent bubbles from forming during deep-frying. Pat to dry. Rub soy sauce on the pork skin; marinate for 5-10 minutes; retain marinade.

❷ Heat the wok then add 2 c. oil. Deep-fry the bacon, skin side down, for 3 minutes, or until the skin is golden brown; remove. Remove the oil from the wok. When cool, cut the bacon into 1/3-inch thick slices. Arrange the slices, skin side down, to line a medium-size bowl. Pack the slices tightly.

❸ Rinse the dried mustard("Mei Gan Tsai")and chop it finely.

❹ Reheat the wok then add 4T. oil. Add the green onion and ginger root; stir-fry until fragrant. Add the"Mei Gan Tsai", retained marinade and ①. Cook for 5 minutes then pour the mixture on top of the slices of bacon. Steam for 1 1/2 hours. Remove and drain the liquid into a bowl by placing a plate over the bowl and tilting the bowl and plate. Invert the bowl on to the serving plate; remove the bowl (See P. 32, Figs. 1, 2). Pour the drained liquid over the top; serve.

Fig.1 Marinate cooked bacon, while hot, with soy sauce for 1 or 2 minutes.

Fig.2 Pat dry the bacon and deep-fry it with the skin side down. Cover the wok to prevent oil from splashing.

Fig.3 Deep-fry the bacon until golden brown; remove the cover when oil stops splashing. Remove the bacon and slice it when cool.

Fig.4 Arrange the slices, skin side down, to line a medium-size bowl

南乳扣肉　Steamed Pork in Preserved Bean Sauce

CANTONESE;
SERVES 12

1 lb. fresh bacon
　(about 3 inches thick)
5 T. soy sauce
1 1/3 lbs. taro root
2 c. oil for frying

1 {
1/2 T. minced garlic clove
1 green onion, cut into 6 pieces
2 squares fermented bean curd
}

2 {
1 T. cooking wine or sherry
1/2 T. sugar
1/2 c. retained broth
}

3 bok choy

❶ Prepare the bacon as in step ❶, page 66. Pare the taro root; cut it into 1"x2" slices.

❷ Heat the wok then add 2 c. oil. Deep-fry the taro root until golden brown; remove. Place the bacon in the wok and deep-fry it, skin side down, for about 3 minutes, or until the skin is golden brown. Remove the bacon and allow to cool; when it is cool cut into thin slices. Remove the oil from the wok.

❸ Reheat the wok then add 1 T. oil. Add ①; stir-fry until fragrant. Add the sliced bacon; stir-fry to mix. Add marinade and ②; cook for 2 minutes. Remove the bacon; retain the liquid.

❹ In a medium-size, heatproof bowl, alternately arrange the taro root and bacon slices, skin side down; pack pieces securely into the bowl. Place the remaining ingredients in the middle. Pour the retained liquid over the sliced bacon; steam for 1 1/2 hours or until soft. Remove the bowl from the steamer. Put a plate on the bowl and tilt them to drain the liquid; invert the bowl onto the plate (See P. 32, Figs. 1, 2). Remove the bowl and pour the drained liquid on the bacon. Garnish with cooked vegetables.

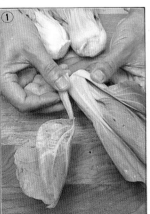 

Fig.1　Remove the outer leaves of the bok choy.

Fig.2　Halve or quarter each stalk lengthwise, depending on the thickness. Blanch the bok choy in boiling water. Remove and plunge into cold water; remove and drain when cool. Stir-fry in hot oiled wok and arrange around the plate before serving.

粉蒸排骨 Steamed Spareribs with Sweet Potato

SERVES 6

① 1 lb. pork back ribs
1 T. each: soy sauce, sweet bean paste, cooking wine or sherry
1 t. each: hot bean paste, sugar dash of black pepper
1/2 T. each: chopped ginger root, garlic clove
1 1/2 T. water
1 pkg. "Jen rou fen" (1/4 cup)
1 c. sweet potato, peeled, cut into bite-size pieces
2 T. chopped green onion

❶ Cut the ribs into 24 pieces; add ① ; mix and marinate for 30 minutes. Add "Jen rou fen"; mix.

❷ Line the bottom of a steamer with the sweet potato; place the ribs on top of the sweet potatoes. Steam for 40 minutes. Remove to a serving platter; sprinkle with the green onion.

■ "Jen rou fen" is a special type of prepared meat-flavored rice powder available in packages at many Chinese markets.

Fig.1 Cut the ribs into pieces.

Fig.2 Add ① and mix. Add "Jen rou fen" and mix.

68

京都排骨　Ching Du Pork Black Ribs

CANTONESE;
SERVES 6

1 lb. pork back ribs
① {
3/4 t. each: salt, sugar
1/2 T. cooking wine or sherry
1/2 T. chopped garlic clove
1 1/2 T. cornstarch
}
oil for frying
② {
1 T. worcestershire sauce
1 1/2 T. ketchup
1/2 T. sugar
1 1/2 T. water
dash of sesame oil
}

❶ Cut the ribs into 15 pieces; mix with ①. Add cornstarch and mix thoroughly.

❷ Heat the wok then add oil. Deep-fry the ribs over medium heat for about 4 minutes, or until golden brown; remove. Reheat the oil; deep-fry the ribs again for 1 minute. Remove and drain.

❸ Bring ② to a boil. Add deep-fried ribs; stir-fry over high heat until liquid has almost completely evaporated. Remove and serve.

■ Worcestershire sauce may be substituted with 2 t. soy sauce and 1 t. white vinegar.

Pork Ribs with Five-spice Powder

6 pork ribs (about 1 lb.)

① {
Use ingredients ① of "Ching Du Pork Back Ribs"
1/3 t. five-spice powder
1 1/2 T. cornstarch
}

oil

② {
2 T. each: soy sauce, sugar
2 T. each: vinegar, garlic clove (mashed)
}

❶ Use a meat mallet to tenderize the pork ribs. Mix with ①.

❷ Heat the wok then add oil. Deep-fry the pork ribs until golden brown and cooked; remove. Sprinkle with ② while pork ribs are still hot.

豆豉排骨　　Steamed Pork Back Ribs with Black Bean Sauce

CANTONESE;
SERVES 6

1 lb. pork back ribs

① {
1/2 T. cooking wine or sherry
2 T. soy sauce
1/2 T. sugar
1 T. cornstarch
dash of sesame oil
}

② {
1 1/2 T. fermented black beans
1/2 T. each: chopped garlic clove,
　　　　　　ginger root
1 T. chopped green onion
1 hot red pepper, thinly sliced
}

❶ Cut the ribs into 20 pieces; add ① and mix thoroughly. Add ②
and mix thoroughly.
❷ Place the ribs in a heatproof dish and steam for 20 minutes.
Remove and serve.

Steamed Ground Beef or Pork with Pickled Cucumber

2/3 lb. ground beef or pork

① {
2/3 c. chopped pickled cucumber
3 T. pickled cucumber liquid
1 T. cooking wine
1/2 T. chopped garlic
}

② {
2 T. pickled cucumber liquid
2 T. soy sauce
}

● Mix the meat with ① Form the meat into a thick patty and
put it on a plate. Sprinkle with ②. Steam over boiling water for 30 minutes.

咖哩排骨　Curried Fried Pork Back Ribs

CANTONESE;
SERVES 6

① 1 lb. pork back ribs
1/2 T. each: cooking wine or sherry, curry powder
1/2 T. each: chopped garlic clove, sugar
1 T. soy sauce
1 t. salt
1 egg yolk
1 1/2 T. cornstarch

❶ Cut ribs into 12 pieces; mix with ① and marinate for 1 hour. Turn ribs over occasionally during marinating time.

❷ Heat the wok then add 3 T. oil. Place the ribs in the wok; fry over low heat for about 6 minutes. Fry both sides of ribs until they are golden brown. Remove to a serving plate; serve.

Fig.1　Fry the marinated meat over low heat.

Fig.2　Fry both sides of the ribs, over low heat, until golden brown. Maintain low heat during frying so that the inside of the ribs will cook.

冰糖排骨　Spareribs Cooked with Rock Sugar　SERVES 6

- 1 1/2 lb. back side ribs
- ① { 1 T. cooking wine or sherry
  1 oz. rock sugar or
  2 T. sugar
  3 T. white vinegar
  4 T. soy sauce

- ● Wash the ribs and cut them into small pieces. Place them in a pot. Add ingredients ①; cover and cook over low heat for 40 minutes, or until the liquid has almost completely evaporated. Remove to a serving plate and serve.
- ■ When cooking the meat, stir occasionally. If the liquid has not almost completely evaporated after 40 minutes of cooking, turn the heat to high and stir until the liquid has almost completely evaporated.

Roast Pork

- ● See p. 66, "Steamed Pork with 'Mei Gan Tsai'". Ingredients and directions are the same except for the "Mei Gan Tsai".
- ■ Garnish the roast pork with cooked vegetables. Serve pork with vegetables to reduce oiliness.

雪菜肉絲 Stir-fried Shredded Meat with Pickled Rape SERVES 6

① 1/2 lb. pork tenderloin,beef, or chicken
meat
1/2 T. cooking wine or sherry
3/4 T. soy sauce
1 T. water
3/4 T. cornstarch
1/2 c. oil for frying
1 c. each: chopped pickled rape,
shredded bamboo shoot

② 1 T. each: cooking wine or sherry,
soy sauce
dash of sugar
1/2 t. sesame oil
4 T. chopped green onion

❶ Shred the meat; mix with ① . Add 1T. oil to meat and mix before frying so that the shredded meat will separate easily during frying.

❷ Heat the wok then add oil. Stir-fry the meat and remove. This is precooking. Remove the oil from wok. Reheat the wok then add 1T. oil. Stir-fry pickled rape; move the pickled rape aside. Add 1 T. oil; Stir-fry the bamboo shoot; add shredded meat and ② (include the pickled rape in the mixture). Turn the heat to high and quicklly stir-fry; remove and serve.

Fig.1 Pickled rape:Select 1 lb. kai choy or rape. Wash it and allow it to dry. Sprinkle it with 1 T. salt.

Fig.2 Rub the kai choy until it is soft. Marinate it for at least 1 day.

73

魚香肉絲　Stir-frid Shredded Meat with Fish Flavor

2/3 lb. pork tenderloin, beef, or cicken meat

① { 1/2 T. cooking wine or sherry
1 T. each: soy sauce, cornstarch
1 1/2 T. water

1/2 c. oil for frying

② { 1 t. hot chili paste
1 T. each: chopped green onion, ginger
root, and garlic cloves

5 chopped water chestnuts
4 T. copped wood ears

③ { 1/2 t. each: cooking wine or sherry, white vinegar
1 1/2 T. soy sauce, 2 1/2 T. water
1 t. each: sugar, cornstarch
dash of sesame oil

❶ Shred the meat; mix with ①. Add 2 T.oil and stir be
fore frying so that the shredded meat will separate
easily during frying.

❷ Heat the wok then add oil. Stir-fry the meat; remove
(precooking). Remove the oil from the wok.

❸ Heat the wok then add 2T. oil. Stir-fry ② until fra
grant. Add water chestnuts and wood ears; stir to
mix. Return the meat to the wok and add ingre
dient ③. Turn heat to high; quickly stir to mix
Remove and serve.

Fig.1　Remove the white membrane from the pork then slice the pork

Fig.2　Shred the sliced pork. It is preferable to use pork tenderloi
for this dish.

京醬肉絲 Shredded Pork with Sweet Bean Paste

PEKING;
SERVES 6

2/3 lb. pork tenderloin or beef
① { 1/2 T. cooking wine or sherry
1 T. each: soy sauce, cornstarch
1 1/2 T. water
1/2 c. oil for frying
② { 1 1/2 T. sweet bean paste
1/2 T. cooking wine or sherry
1 T. soy sauce
2/3 T. sugar
1/2 t. cornstarch
1/2 c. shredded green onions

❶ Shred the meat, mix with ① . Add 2 T. oil and stir before frying so that the shredded meat will separate easily during frying. Mix ② in a bowl and set aside for later use. Soak the shredded green onions in water for about 5 minutes; remove. Place the onions on two sides of the plate or line the bottom of the plate.

❷ Heat the wok then add the oil. Stir-fry the meat then remove it (precooking). Remove the oil from the wok. Reheat the wok and add 1 T. oil. Stir-fry ② until fragrant. Add the meat; stir-fry to mix; remove. Place it on the serving plate. Before serving, mix the green onions with the meat together.

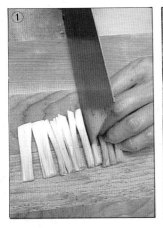

Fig. 1 Cut the green onions to uniform lengths. Cut the lengths into 2-inch pieces then cut them in half lengthwise.

Fig. 2 Shred the green onion.

花瓜肉絲 Stir-fried Pork with Pickled Cucumber

SERVES 6

① 2/3 lb. shredded pork tenderloin
{ 2 1/2 T. pickled cucumber liquid
    (reserved from can)
  1/2 T. cooking wine or sherry
  1 T. cornstarch
1/2 c. oil for frying
1 green onion, cut into 6 pieces
3/4 c. canned Wei-Chuan pickled
    cucumbers, shredded
② { 2 T. pickled cucumber liquid
    2 T. soy sauce

❶ Mix the shredded meat with ① .Add 2 T. oil to the meat and mix before frying so that the shredded meat will separate easily during frying.
❷ Heat the wok then add oil; stir-fry the meat and remove it (precooked). Remove the oil. Reheat the wok then add 1 T. oil; stir-fry green onion until fragrant. Add meat, pickled cucumbers, and ② . Turn heat to high; stir quickly to mix. Remove and serve.

Fig.1 Take the pickled cucumber out of the can.
Fig.2 Shred the pickled cucumber.

榨菜肉絲 Stir-fried Shredded Meat with Szechuan Mustard Greens SERVES 6

1/2 lb. shredded pork tenderloin, beef, or chicken meat

① { 1/2 T. cooking wine or sherry, 1 T. water
3/4 T. each: soy sauce, cornstarch
1/2 c. oil for frying

② { 1 T. each: green onion, ginger root, hot red pepper } shredded
1/4 c. bell pepper, shredded

③ { 1/2 c. Szechuan pickled mustard greens } Shredded
1 c. bamboo shoot } precooked
1/4 c. carrot

④ { 1/2 t. salt, 1 t. cornstarch, 1 1/2 T. water
dash of sesame oil, black pepper

❶ Mix meat with ①. Add 2 T. oil; mix before frying so that the shredded meat will separate easily during frying.

❷ Heat the wok then add oil; stir-fry meat until cooked; remove (precooked). Remove the oil from the wok. Reheat the wok then add 2 T. oil. Add ② in order given; stir after each addition. Add ③; stir to mix. Add meat and ④; turn heat to high and stir quickly to mix. Remove and serve.

■ Before using, Szechuan pickled mustard greens may be soaked in water for 3 minutes so that they will be cripsier.

Fig.1 Slice the Szechuan pickled mustard greens.

Fig.2 Shred the Szechuan pickled mustard greens.

香干肉絲 Stir-fried Meat with Pressed Bean Curd SERVES 6

1/2 lb. shredded tenderloin
① { 1/2 T. each: cooking wine or sherry water
3/4 T. each: soy sauce, cornstarch
1/2 c. oil for frying
1 t. green onin, cut into match-like strips
3/4 c. shredded bamboo shoots
1 c. shredded five-spice pressed bean curd
② { 1/2 T. each: cooking wine or sherry, sugar
1 1/2 T. soy sauce
dash of pepper
dash of sesame oil

❶ Mix the shredded meat with ① . Before stir-frying add 2T. oil and mix so that the meat will separate easily during frying.
❷ Heat the wok then add oil. Stir-fry the shredded meat until cooked (precooked). Remove and drain the meat. Remove the oil from the wok.
❸ Reheat the wok. Add 2T. oil. Stir-fry the green onions until fragrant. Add bamboo shoots and pressed bean curd; stir to mix. Add the meat and ② . Turn the heat to high; stir quickly to mix. Transfer to a serving platter and serve.
■ The saltiness of the pressed bean curd may depend upon the manufacturer; therefore, adapt to taste by varying the amount of soy sauce in ingredients

Stir-fried Beef with Pickled Mustard Cabbage

1/2 lb. shredded beef
① { 1/2 T. each: cooking wine, water
3/4 T. each: soy sauce, cornstarch
1 c. shredded pickled mustard cabbage
2 c. bean sprouts
6 pieces green onion, 1 inch long
3 T. oil

② { 1 T. cooking wine
1/2 T. sugar
dash of black pepper
1/2 t. each: salt, sesame oil
2 T. water
2 T. cornstarch

❶ Soak the pickled mustard cabbage in water for 5 minutes. Squeeze out the excess water.
❷ Mix the beef with ① . Stir-fry the beef until cooked; remove.
❸ Heat the wok then add 3 T. oil. Stir-fry the green onions. Add pickled mustard cabbage, bean sprouts, beef, and ② . Turn the heat to high; stir quickly to mix and remove.
■ Beef and pickled mustard cabbage may be placed over the fried won ton skins.

肉絲拉皮 Tossed Pork and Shredded Egg Sheets

PEKING; SERVES 6

2/3 c. shredded pork loin, beef, or chicken (about 1/3 lb.)

① { 1/2 T. each: cooking wine or sherry, soy sauce
1/2 T. cornstarch

1 c. bean thread sheet, cut into 1/2"-wide strips

2 eggs, scrambled and pan fried to a thin pancake shape

4 T. copped coriander (cilantro)

② { 1 T. each: hot mustard, soy sauce, white vinegar
1/2 t. each: salt, sesame oil
1 t. sugar, 2 T. water
dash of black pepper

❶ Mix the shredded meat with ① ; set aside for later use. Quickly blanch the bean thread strips, stir to separate the strips Remove and drain; place on a serving plate. Separately add ② and mix after each addition. Set aside for later use.

❷ Heat the wok then add 4 T. oil; stir-fry the shredded meat; place the meat in the middle of the shredded bean thread strips. Shred the egg sheet and place the shreds on both sides of the meat. Garnish with coriander. Before serving, pour ② over the meat and egg sheet shreds; serve.

■ Finely shredded cucumber may be used to line the platter.

■ To prepare: dried bean thread sheets, see p. 35; hot mustard, see p. 17.

  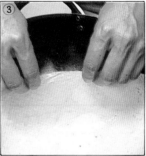

ig. 1 To make an egg sheet (The egg sheet will cook easily and hold better if a mixture of 1 Tbsp. of cornstarch and 1 Tbsp. of water is added to the beaten egg.): Heat the wok then grease it with a paper towel or cloth.

igs. 2. 3 Turn the heat to low and pour in the beaten eggs. Rotate the wok slowly to form a pancake-like sheet. When the egg sheet is firm, take it gently from the edge and turn it over to cook other side. Remove.

紫菜肉捲　Nori Rolls with Chopped Pork

TAIWANESE;
SERVES 6

① {
2/3 lb. ground pork
4 oz. shrimp paste or fish paste
1 egg
3/4 t. salt
dash of black pepper
1 T. cooking wine or sherry
1 1/2 T. cornstarch
2 T. chopped green.onion
}
4 sheets nori
oil for frying

❶ Mix togetherthe ground pork, shrimp paste, ingredients①, and onion (filling). Divide into 4 portions.

❷ Place 1 portin of filling at one end of a sheet of nori; roll it up to the shape of a baton. Repeat this procedure with the other three portions.

❸ Heat the wok then add oil. Deep-fry rolls over medium heat for 5 minutes; remove and drain. Slice the rolls into small pieces; arrange them on a serving plate; serve.

To prepare shrimp paste: Rinse and devein shrimp; drain. Use the flat side of a cleaver to mash the shrimp; then chop finely. Put mashed shrimp in a bowl and stir until the mixture becomes sticky. See p. 81 for fish paste.

■ The dish may be served hot or cold. Szechuan Peppercorn salt or ketchup may be used for dipping before eating. To prepare Szechuan Peppercorn salt, see p. 17.

Fig.1　Place a portion of shrimp paste at one end of a sheet of nori.

Fig.2　Roll up the nori to the shape of a baton.

腐皮肉捲　Bean Curd Rolls with Chopped Pork

TAIWANESE
SERVES 6

4 oz. each: ground pork, fish paste
　　　　　　(or shrimp paste)

① {
1 t. cooking wine or sherry
1/4 t. salt, 3 T. water
1 T. cornstarch

2 leaves Chinese broccoli,
　　precooked
2 sheets nori
2 sheets bean curd skin
6 raw salty egg yolks

} 2"x8"
pieces

② {
1 egg
3 T. flour
} mix

dash of Szechuan peppercorn salt
oil for fry

❶ Mix ground pork, fish paste, and ① together to make the filling. Divide the mixture in half.

❷ Spread some mixture of ② on a bean curd skin; place a sheet of nori on top of the mixture. Spread one portion of the filling on the nori then place one leaf of Chinese broccoli on the filling. Take three salty egg yolks and crumble them along one end of the nori. Roll to form a baton. Follow the same procedure with the other half of filling.

❸ Heat the wok then add oil. Deep-fry the rolls over medium heat for 4 minutes, or until golden brown and the skin becomes crispy. Remove and drain. Cut the rolls into 1-inch pieces; place on a serving platter. Use Szechuan peppercorn salt for dipping.

To prepare fish paste: Clean the fish meat and chop it finely. Stir until it becomes sticky. Use as directed. Fish paste may be purchased ready made.

■ To prepare Szechuan peppercorn salt, see p. 17.

Fig.1 Spread some mixture ② on a bean curd skin.

Fig.2 Place a sheet of nori on top of the mixture. Place one portion of filling on the nori. Place a leaf of Chinese broccoli on the filling then place the salty egg yolks on the Chinese broccoli. Roll it up to the shape of a baton.

碧緑肉捲　Stir-fried Pork Rolls with Broccoli

CANTONESE;
SERVES 6

	2/3 lb. pork loin
①	1/3 t. salt
	1/2 T. coking wine or sherry
	1 egg yolk
	1/2 T. cornstarch

cornstarch for coating
oil for frying
3 Chinese blackmushrooms
12 1 1/2 inch pieces green onion

	1/2 T. each: cooking wine or sherry, soy sauce
②	2 T. water
	1/3 t. salt
	1 t. each: sugar, cornstarch

dash of sesame oil

❶ Cut pork loin into 12 slices. Use a meat mallet to tenderize the meat. (See p. 83, Figs. 1, 2). Mix with ① and marinate until ready for use. soak the black mushrooms in water until soft;cut into 12 julienne strips. Place 1 slice of meat on the working surface. Place 1 piece each of black mushroom and green onion at one end of the meat then roll it up. Place the roll in a bowl of cornstarch to coat.

❷ Remove any wilted leaves from the broccoli; cut into long pieces. Cook in boiling water; remove and plunge them into a bowl of cold water.

❸ Heat the wok then add oil. Deep-fry the meat rolls for 3 minutes or until golden brown. Remove and drain. Remove the oil from the wok.

❹ Reheat the wok then add 2 T. oil. Stir-fry broccoli; add the meat rolls and② . Turn heat to high; quickly stir to mix. Remove to a serving dish and serve.

Fig.1　Place a piece of black mushroom and green onion on a slice of meat and roll it up.

Fig.2　Coat the meat with cornstarch; hold the meat roll tightly so that the cornstarch will stick firmly.

葱爆里肌　Stir-fried Pork with Green Onions

PEKING;
SERVES 6

①
- 2/3 lb. pork tenderloin
- 1 T. soy sauce
- 1/2 T. each: cooking wine or sherry, water
- 1/2 T. each: chopped garlic, sugar
- 1 T. cornstarch

- 1 c. green onion, cut into 2-inch pieces

②
- 2 T. soy sauce
- 1/2 T. sugar

❶ Cut the meat into 2/3-inch thick slices. Tenderize the meat with a meat mallet; mix with ①

❷ Heat the wok then add 3T. oil; fry the meat until both sides are golden brown; move the meat aside. Stir-fry the onions until fragrant. Add ingredients ② ; return the meat to the center of the wok and stir quickly to mix in onions. Remove and serve.

Fig.1 Cut the meat into slices 2/3 inch thick.

Fig.2 Tenderize the meat with a meat mallet.

83

| 蜜汁火腿 | **Glazed Ham Slics** | HUNAN;
SERVES 12 |

2/3 lb. precooked Chinese ham
    cut into 24 slices, 3 inches wide

4 oz. red dates

① { 6 T. rock sugar or
    granulated sugar
  2 T. cooking wine or sherry or
    fermented rice wine } mix

② { 1 t. cornstarch
  1 T. water } mix

1/2 loaf white bread, not sliced

❶ Layer the sliced ham in a medium-size bowl, pack tightly. Spread the dates on top of the slices of ham. Add mixture①; steam for 2 hours. Remove the bowl of sliced ham and place a large plate over the bowl; tilt to drain the liquid (retain liquid fo future use). Invert the bowl on to the plate and remove the bowl. (See p. 32, Figs. 1, 2)

❷ Bring the retained liquid to a boil, if liquid does not equal 1 cup, add water. Add mixture ② to thicken; stir and pour over the sliced ham.

❸ Cut off the crust from the bread; cut it into slices 3/5" thick. Do not cut through the first slice; cut through the second slice (a pocket is formed). Continue cutting the entire loaf in this manner. Steam the slices of bread to soften them. Place the slices of ham between the slices of bread to serve as sandwiches.

■ If the ham is too salty steam the ham to remove its saltiness. Cover the ham with water and steam for 30 minutes. Discard the water and proceed with recipe.

■ If available, Kuei Hua Sauce may be added to ① to add taste.

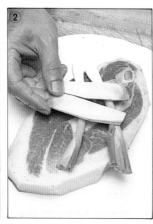

Fig.1 Trim the skin from the ham.

Fig.2 Place green onions and ginger root on the ham. Steaming the meat before slicing it prevents the meat from curling.

冬筍臘肉 Spicy Dried Pork with Bamboo Shoots

HUNAN;
SERVES 6

1/2 lb. sliced spicy dried pork
1 c. sliced bamboo shoot
1 c. fresh garlic, sliced diagonally
   (separate white and green
   pieces)

① { 1 T. fermented black beans
    1 hot red pepper, sliced
    6 slices ginger root

② { 1 T. cooking wine or sherry
    1/4 t. salt
    dash of sesame oil

● Heat the wok then add 1/2 T. oil. Stir-fry pieces of pork. Remove the meat to a dish. Add ① ;stir until fragrant. Add the white part of the garlic and the bamboo shoot; stir to mix. Add ingredients ② ; stir to mix. Add the sliced pork and the green part of the garlic; mix thoroughly. Remove and serve.

Fig.1 Trim the skin from the pork strip.

Fig.2 Slice the pork strip diagonally.

酸菜炒肉丁　Stir-fried Pork with Pickled Mustard Greens

SERVES 6

1/2 lb. pork loin, cubed
(beef loin or chicken meat)

① { 1 t. cooking wine or sherry
1/4 t. salt
3/4 T. cornstarch

1 c. pickled mustard greens, diced

② { 1 T. each: garlic clove, chopped
hot red pepper, diced

③ { 1 T. each: cooking wine or sherry
soy bean paste,
soy sauce
1 t. sugar
dash of sesame oil

1/2 c. roasted peanuts

❶ Mix the meat with ① ; mix thoroughly and let stand until ready for use. Mix ③ in a bowl and save for later use.

❷ Heat the wok then add 4 T. oil. Stir-fry the meat until cooked; remove and drain (this is precooking); set aside. Stir-fry ② until fragrant. Add pickled mustard greens and stir to mix; add meat and ③ ; stir to mix. Add the roasted peanuts and mix together quickly; remove to a serving plate and serve.

Fig.1 Peel off the leaves of the pickled mustard green.

Fig.2 Cut the leaves into strips then dice them coursely.

砂鍋獅子頭   Lion's Head Casserole

3 1/3 lbs. nappa cabbage
1 lb. ground pork
① {
3/4 t. each: rice wine, salt
dash of sesame oil
dash of black pepper
1 t each: green onion } chopped
         ginger root
1 egg, 4 T. water, 1/2 T. cornstarch
}
② {
1/2 T. each: soy sauce, water } mix
1/2 T. cornstarch
}
③ {
1 T. soy sauce
1/2 t. salt
}

❶ Rinse the cabbage lightly; remove and retain, 4 outer leaves cut remaining cabbage into 2-inch pieces.

❷ Mix the ground pork with ① then divide it into 4 portions. Roll each portion into a ball.

❸ Heat wok then add 4 T. oil; dip each meatball into the mixture ②. Remove then fry the meatballs until all sides are golden brown; remove. Deep-fry the pieces of cabbage and add 1 c. water; cover and cook for 5 minutes or until soft. Line the bottom of a casserole dish with the cabbage. Place the meatballs on top of the cabbage. Cover the meatballs with the 4 cabbage leaves reserved in step ❶. Add ③; cover and turn the heat to low. Cook for 1 hour.

■ Bean curd, Chinese black mushrooms, bamboo shoots, etc. may be added to ground pork to taste.

Fig.1 Mix the ground pork with ① then divide it into 4 portions. Roll each portion into a ball. Dip each meatball in mixture ②

Fig.2 Fry the meatball until completely golden brown.

紅燒牛尾　Ox Tail Cooked in Red Sauce

SERVES 12

1 ox tail (about 2 lbs.)
1/2 brown onion, cut into
　bite-size pieces
1 tomato, cut into bite-size pieces

①
- 3 T. cooking wine or sherry
- 2 T. soy sauce
- 1 T. soy bean paste
- 2 T. ketchup
- 1/2 T. sugar
- 2 c. water

② { 1 T. water / 1 t. cornstarch } mix

❶ Wash the ox tail then cut it into pieces at the joints. If desired, large pieces may be cut lengthwise. Place the pieces of ox tail in boiling water; cook for 2 minutes.Remove and drain.

❷ Heat the wok then add 3 T. oil. Stir-fry the brown onions until fragrant. Add tomato and stir to mix. Add ① and pieces of ox tail. Bring to a boil; cover and turn heat to low. Cook for 1 1/2 to 2 hours, or until the meat is tender and the liquid is reduced to 1/2 cup. Add mixture ② to thicken; stir. Transfer to a serving plate and serve.

■ When cooking the ox tail, stir occasionally to prevent burning. If the liquid has not reduced to 1/2 cup after 2 hours of cooking, turn the heat to high and stir until the liquid has reduced to 1/2 cup.

Fig.1　Cut the ox tail at the joints. Large pieces may be cut in half.

Fig.2　Cook in boiling water for 2 minutes to remove the odd smell and to clean the meat so that the broth may remain clear.

沙茶牛肉　　Beef with Sa Tsa Sauce

CANTONESE;
SERVES 6

2/3 lb. beef, thinly sliced

① { 1/2 T. each: cooking wine or sherry, water
1 T. each: soy sauce, cornstarch

1/2 c. oil for frying

1 brown onion, cut into bite-size pieces

② { 3 T. Sa Tsa Sauce
2 T. soy sauce
1/2 T. sugar

❶ Mix the beef with ①. Before stir-frying, add 2 T. oil and mix. The meat will separately easily during frying.

❷ Heat the wok then add oil. Stir-fry the meat until it is cooked (this is precooking). Remove the beef, then remove the oil from the wok. Reheat the wok then add 2 T. oil. Stir-fry the onions until fragrant. Return the beef to the wok and add ②. Turn the heat to high quickly stir to mix the ingredients. Transfer to a serving plate and serve.

Fig.1 Halve the beef if it is too thick.

Fig.2 Slice the beef across the grain of the meat so that it will be tender after frying.

雪豆牛肉　Sliced Beef with Snow Peas

① 1/2 lb. beef tenderloin or flank steak
1/2 T. each: cooking wine or sherry, water
3/4 T. each: soy sauce, cornstarch

1/2 c. oil for frying
1 green onion, cut into 6 pieces
6 slices of ginger root

② 1 c. Chinese pea pods
1/3 c. button mushroom
12 slices bamboo shoot

③ 1 1/2 T. oyster sauce, 1 T. soy sauce
1/2 T. cooking wine or sherry
2 T. water
dash of sesame oil, black pepper
1 t. each: sugar, cornstarch

❶ Slice the beef; mix with ① ; add 1 T. oil and mix. The meat will separate easily during frying.

❷ Heat the wok then add oil. Stir-fry the meat until it is almost cooked (precooked) remove. Remove the oil from the wok. Reheat the wok then add 2 T. oil. Stir-fry the green onion and ginger root until fragrant. Add ② and stir; add beef and ③ . Turn heat to high and stir-fry quickly to mix. Remove to a serving plate and serve.

■ If oyster sauce is unavailable, increase the soy sauce to 2 1/2 T.

Fig.1 Select small Chinese snow peas. Pull off the string of the peas.

Fig.2 For a more elegant appearance, trim the ends to form a "v".

時菜牛肉 Beef with Nappa Cabbage in Oyster Sauce CANTONESE; SERVES 6

① {
1/2 lb. beef tenderloin or flank steak
1/2 T. each: cooking wine or sherry water
3/4 T. each: soy sauce, cornstarch
}

1/2 c.oil for frying
2/3 lb. nappa cabbage, cut into bite-size pieces
1 green onion, cut into 6 pieces
6 slices of ginger root

② {
1 1/2 t. oyster sauce
1 T. soy sauce
1/2 T. cooking wine or sherry
2 T. water
dash of sugar, sesame oil
dash of black pepper, 1 t. cornstarch
}

❶ Slice the beef; add ① and mix. Set aside for later use. Before frying, add 1 T. oil and mix so that the slices of beef will separate easily during frying.

❷ Heat the wok then add 3 T. oil; stir-fry the cabbage with 1/4 t. salt until it becomes limp. Remove and drain. Place on a serving plate.

❸ Heat the wok then add oil; stir-fry the meat slices until almost cooked (this is precooking); remove. Remove the oil from the wok. Reheat the wok then add 2 T. oil; stir-fry the green onions and ginger root until fragrant. Add beef and ②. Turn heat to high and stir quickly to mix. Remove and place on top of the cabbage; serve.

■ If oyster sauce is unavailable, increase the soy sauce to 2 1/2 t. nappa cabbage may be substituted with any kind of green vegetables.

Beef with Chinese Broccoli

● Ingredients and directions are the same as for "Beef with Nappa Cabbage in Oyster Sauce" except substitute the cabbage with Chinese broccoli.

干扁牛肉   Stir-fried Beef with Vegetables

SZECHUAN;
SERVES 6

1 lb. shredded beef tenderloin or
    flank steak
1 c. oil for frying
1/2 c. shredded carrot
1/2 c. celery, cut into 2-inch pieces
    and shredded finely lengthwise

① { 1/2 T. hot bean paste
    1/2 T. each: ginger root } chopped
                 green onion

② { 1 T. soy sauce
    1/2 T. each: cooking wine or sherry,
                 sugar
    dash of sesame oil
    1/3 t. Szechuan peppercorn powder

❶ Heat the wok then add oil. Deep-fry the shredded beef for 12 minutes; remove the beef and drain. Remove the oil from the wok and clean.

❷ Reheat the wok then add 1 1/2 T. oil. Stir-fry ① until fragrant. Add shredded carrot and celery; stir-fry until tender. Add beef and ② ; stir to mix. Remove to a serving plate; serve.

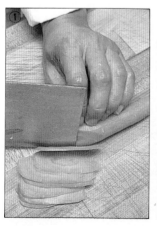

Fig. 1   Pare the carrot and diagonally cut it into thin slices.

Fig. 2   Shred the sliced carrot.

家常牛肉　Family-style Stir-fried Beef

SERVES 6

① 1/2 lb. beef tenderloin
1/2 T. cooking wine or sherry, 1 T. water
3/4 T. each: cornstarch, soy sauce
1/2 c. oil for frying

② 2 green onions, cut into 4 pieces and
shredded finely lengthwise
5 garlic cloves, mashed
1 T. shredded ginger root
2 hot red peppers, shredded
1/2 c. shredded carrots
1 1/2 c. shredded celery, cut into 2-inch pieces
and shredded finely lengthwise

③ 1/2 T. each: cooking wine or sherry, sugar,
white vinegar, soy sauce
1/4 t. salt, 1 t. cornstarch, 1 T. water

❶ Shred the beef into 1/4-inch strips; mix with ①. Add 2 T. oil and mix before frying. The shredded meat will separate easily during frying.

❷ Heat the wok then add oil. Stir-fry the shredded beef until it changes color; remove and drain (this is precooking.) Remove the oil from the wok.

❸ Reheat the wok then add 2 T. oil. Stir-fry ② until fragrant. Add the carrots and celery; stir-fry them. Return the meat to the wok; add ③. Turn the heat to high; stir and mix quickly. Transfer to a serving plate and serve.

Fig.1　To marinate the beef: Mix the cooking wine, water, and soy sauce with the beef; add cornstarch and mix. If mixture is too dry, add a little water or egg white.

Fig.2　Add 2 T. oil and mix before frying so that the meat will separate easily during frying.

麻辣牛筋　　Sliced Beef Tendons

SZECHUAN;
SERVES 6

① 1 lb. beef tendons
2 T. soy sauce
1/2 c. water
dash of chopped coriander
2 green onions, sliced diagonally

② 3 T. soy sauce
1 T. each: hot pepper oil,
          sesame oil
2 t. each: sugar, white vinegar
1/2 t. salt

❶ Clean the beef tendons by rinsing them. Place the tendons and ① in a heatproof bowl. Steam for 4 hours, or until tender. Remove the bowl of tendons from the steamer. Place the tendons in another bowl and refrigerate. When cool, remove and cut into thin slices.

❷ Mix the sliced tendons with the chopped coriander, green onion, and ② ; place on a serving plate and serve.

Fig.1 Steamed tendons may be put in a plastic bag and refrigerated.

Fig.2 Tendons will be easier to slice if they are chilled.

| 中式牛排 | **Chinese-style Beef Steak** | CANTONESE; SERVES 6 |

① 1 lb. beef tenderloin
   2 T. soy sauce
   1 T. water
   1 T. each: cooking wine, or sherry
              cornstarch

   1 brown onion, shredded
② 1 T. each: sugar, white vinegar
   1 1/2 T. ketchup
   2 T. soy sauce
   3 T. water
   1 hot red pepper, sliced diagonally

❶ Cut the beef into 6 slices. Tenderize the meat with a meat mallet to make each piece about 1/2 inch thick (See P. 83, Figs. 1. 2). Mix the meat with ① and marinate for 1 hour.

❷ Heat the wok then add 2 T. oil. Fry the meat until both sides are golden brown; cook until medium done. Remove the meat; drain. Remove the oil from the wok.

❸ Reheat the wok then add 3 T. oil. Stir-fry the brown onion until fragrant. Add ② and bring to a boil. Add the meat; turn the heat to high and mix quickly. Remove to a serving plate and serve.

■ To make the meat more tender, add 1/2 t. baking sada to ① .

■ Pork tenderloin or pork chops may be used for this recipe.

Fig.1 Heat the wok then add oil. Fry the meat until it is golden brown

Fig.2 Turn the meat over. Fry other side until it is golden brown

酸菜肚絲 Stir-fried Pork Maws with Pickled Mustard Greens

TAIWANESE;
SERVES 6

① { 1 T. hot red pepper
2 T. tender ginger root } shredded
3 T. green onions

1 c. pickled mustard greens
1/2 c. bamboo shoots } shredded
2 c. precooked pork maw

② { 1/2 T. each: cooking wine or sherry,
soy sauce
1/4 t. salt
dash of sesame oil

■ Heat the wok then add 3 T. oil; add ① and stir-fry until fragrant. Add pickled mustard greens, bamboo shoots, pork maw, and ②. Stir-fry for 2 minutes; remove and serve.

■ Pickled mustard greens may be substituted with fine strips of celery.

To prepare pork mow:

❶ Wash the pork maw and remove any scum. Make a 4-inch cut along the side of the maw then turn it inside out. Rub 1 T. salt and 1 T. vinegar on the surface to scrub off and remove the stickness. Rinse thoroughly with fresh water. Place the maw in a pot of water, to cover, and cook for 3 minutes, remove. Use a knife to scrape the white membrane off the maw. Discard the water.

❷ Put 6 c. water in pot. Add 2 green onions, 2 slices of ginger root, 1 T. cooking wine, and the pork maw. Bring to a boil. Boil for 1 1/2 hours or until the maw is tender. The broth may be retained for other uses.

Fig.1 Halve the precooked pork maws lengthwise. Scrape the white membrane off the maws.

Fig.2 Shred the pork maws.

椒麻腰片   **Sliced Kidneys in Hot Sauce**   SZECHUAN; SERVES 6

3 large pork kidneys
1 c. bean thread sheets, cut into
    1/2-inch strips or
    1 c. shredded cucumber

① { 1/2 T. Szechuan peppercorns
    3 T. green onions } chopped finely
    1 T. ginger root }

② { 3 T. soy sauce
    1/4 t. salt
    1 t. sugar
    2 t. white vinegar
    dash of sesame oil

❶ Slice the kidneys horizontally in half; remove the white membrane from the center. Make four or five vertical cuts on the surface of the kidney (do not cut through). Turn the slices of kidney so that the cuts are in a horizontal position. Diagonally cut thin slices along the horizontal cuts to form scalloped edge. Soak the sliced kidney in cold water to clean them.

❷ Place the shredded bean thread strips in hot water; stir quickly to separate. Remove.

❸ Drain the water from the slices of kidney; blanch them in boiling water for about 20 seconds. When the slices of kidney turn white, remove and plunge them into cold water.

❹ Place ① in a bowl and mix with ② (sauce).

❺ Arrange the bean thread strips on a plate; drain the kidney slices and place them on top of the bean thread strips. Pour the sauce over the slices of kidney. Mix before serving.

■ To use dried bean thread sheets see p. 35, Figs. 1, 2.

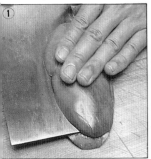 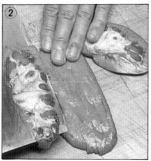 

Fig.1 Slice the kidneys horizontally in half.
Fig.2 Cut off the white membrane from the center.
Fig.3 Make vertical cuts on the surface of the kidney; do not cut through. Turn the slices so that the cuts are in a horizontal position. Diagonally cut thin slices along the horizontal cuts to form scalloped edge.

生炒腰花 Stir-fried Kidney with Assorted Vegetables SERVES 6

① {
3 large pork kidneys
1 green onion, cut into 6 pieces
6 slices ginger root
3 garlic clove, mashed
}

② {
12 Chinese pea pods
12 slices precooked carrot
12 slices precooked bamboo shoots
}

③ {
1 T. each: soy sauce, cooking wine
　　　　　　or sherry
1/2 t. each: salt, sugar, white vinegar
1 t. cornstarch
dash of black pepper, sesame oil
}

❶ Slice each kidney in half horizontally and remove the white membrane from the center. Make 5 or 6 cuts along the width of the kidney; these will form scallops later. Diagonally cut a thin slice along the horizontal cuts, do not through the first two slices, cut through the third slice. (Three slices will be attached.) Continue slicing until the whole kidney has been sliced. Soak the kidney slices in cold water to clean them. Blanch the kidney slices in boiling water for about 20 seconds. Remove them when they turn white; plunge into cold water. Drain thoroughly before stir-frying.

❷ Heat the wok then add 2 T. oil. Stir-fry the kidney slices; remove when the kidney slices are hot, Drain. Discard the oil and water from the wok. Reheat the wok then add 2 T. oil. Stir-fry ① until fragrant. Add ② ; stir briefly. Add kidney slices and ③ ; turn heat to high and quickly stir to mix. Remove and serve.

Fig.1　Clean the pork kidneys(see p. 97, Figs. 1 and 2)Make 5 or 6 vertical cuts along the width of the kidney; do not cut through the first two slices, cut through the third slice.

Fig.2　Soak the kidney slices in cold water for 1 hour. Blanch the slices of kidney in boiling water until they are white; remove.

生炒豬肝 Stir-fried Liver with Assorted Vegetables

SERVES 6

2/3 lb. pork liver
① { 1/2 T. cooking wine or sherry
1 T. soy sauce
1/2 c. oil for frying
② { 1 green onion, cut into 6 pieces
6 slices ginger root
1/2 T. minced garlic clove
③ { 12 slices cucumber
12 slices precooked carrot
12 slices precooked bamboo shoots
④ { 1/3 t. salt
1/2 t. each: sugar, white vinegar
1 1/2 T. water, 1 t. cornstarch
dash of black pepper, sesame oil

❶ Slice the liver into thin slices. Mix in a bowl with ① .
❷ Heat the wok then add oil. Stir-fry the liver to rare; remove. Remove the oil from the wok. Reheat the wok then add 2 T. oil. Stir-fry ② until fragrant. Add ③ ; stir .Add liver and ④ ; turn heat to high and quickly stir-fry to mix. Remove and serve.

Fig.1 Cut long, v-shaped strips around the length of the cucumber.

Fig.2 Slice the cucumber.

燒划水   **Simmered Fish Halves** SHANGHAI;
SERVES 12

1 2/3 lbs. fish halves (tail end)
1 green onion, cut into 6
   1-inch pieces
6 slices ginger root
1 stalk fresh garlic

① ⎰ 3 T. soy sauce
   1 T. sugar
   1 c. water
   dash of black pepper

② ⎰ 1/2 T. cornstarch ⎱ mix
   1 T. water
   1 t. each: white vinegar, sesame oil

❶ Scale and clean the fish. Cut it in half lengthwise to remove bones; cut each half in thirds, do not cut through the tail. (To total 12 sections.)

❷ Cut the garlic into several pieces then shred finely lengthwise. Soak it in water for 5 minutes; remove and drain.

❸ Heat the wok then add 4 T. oil. Stir-fry the green onion and ginger root until fragrant. Add fish, skin side down; fry for 20 seconds, or until golden. Turn the fish over. Add ① ; cover and turn heat to low. Simmer for 5 minutes; when the liquid has reduced to half its original amount, add mixture ② ; stir lightly. Sprinkle with vinegar and sesame oil; place on serving plate. Sprinkle the finely shredded garlic on top; serve.

Fig.1 Cut the fish in half lengthwise to remove the bones.

Fig.2 Cut each half in thirds; do not cut through the tail.

豆瓣魚　Braised Fish with Hot Bean Paste

SZECHUAN;
SERVES 12

① {
1 whole carp (about 1 2/3 lbs.)
1 T. hot bean paste
1 T. each: green onion
　　　　　ginger root　} chopped
　　　　　garlic clove
}

② {
1 T. soy sauce
1/2 T. each: sugar, white vinegar
1/2 t. salt
1 1/2 c. water
}

③ {
1 T. cornstarch　} mix
2 T. water
}

3 T. chopped green onion

❶ Scale and clean the fish. Make a few diagonal cuts through the meat along the spine. The slits allow the sauce to permeate into the fish.

❷ Heat the wok then add 4 T. oil. Swirl the oil around the wok so that three-fourths of the surface is oiled. Hold the fish by the tail and place it on the edge of the wok; gradually lower the fish into the wok. Fry entire fish—head and tail, completely on one side; turn over and completely fry other side until golden. Remove or set aside.

❸ If necessary, add oil to the wok. Stir-fry ① until fragrant. Return the fish to the center of the wok. Add ②; cover and cook over medium heat for about 4 minutes. Turn fish, cover, and cook for about 4 more minutes. When the fish is cooked and the liquid has reduced to half, transfer the fish to a serving plate. Add ③ to thicken; stir. Add green onion and drizzle over the fish.

■ If carp is unavailable, substitute perch, salmon, or sea bass.

Braised Fish with Hot Bean Paste

● Substitute whole fish with fish pieces, include bone, or fish fillets. Other ingredients and directions are the same.

101

糖醋魚   **Sweet and Sour Fish**

CANTONESE;
SERVES 12

① {
1 whole yellow fish (about 1 2/3 lbs.)
1 T. cooking wine or sherry
1 t. salt
1 egg yolk
} mix

1 c. cornstarch, oil for frying

② {
1/2 T. chopped garlic clove
1/2 c. brown onion
1 T. Chinese black mushroom
4 T. each: carrot, bell pepper
} shredded

③ {
6 T. each: sugar, white vinegar,
ketchup, water
1/2 t. salt, 1 1/2 t. cornstarch

shredded green onion
chopped coriander
} for garnish

❶ Scale and clean the fish, if necessary. Hold a cutting knife so that the blade is at a 30° angle. Make diagonal cuts through the meat to the bone at every 1/2 inch on both sides of the fish. Rub fish and inside cuts with mixture ①; marinate for 1/2 hour. Coat fish, including inside of cuts, with egg yolk then with cornstarch before frying. Place the fish on a flat surface, with the spine on top; press lightly so that it will stay upright.

❷ Heat the wok then add oil. Carefully lift the fish by the tail and place it on the edge of the wok. Gently lower the fish into the wok, spine on top. Ladle some hot oil over the fish; this allows the cuts to maintain an "open" position. Turn the heat to high and fry for about 10 minutes, or until the fish is cooked and the skin has become crispy.

❸ Reheat the wok then add 2 T. oil. Stir-fry ② until fragrant. Add ③ and bring to a boil. Add 1 T. oil to make the sauce shiny. Drizzle the sauce over the fish. Garnish with shredded green onion and coriander.

■ Any fish may be used for this recipe.

Fig.1 Make diagonal cuts through the meat, to the bone, at every 1/2 inch on both sides of the fish.

Fig.2 Press cornstarch tightly into the slits to coat the fish.

雞油海鮮 Steamed Pomfret with Ham and Mushroom Slices

CANTONESE;
SERVES 6

① {
1 whole pomfret (about 1 lb.)
1 T. cooking wine or sherry
1/2 T. salt
1 green onion, cut into 6 pieces
2 slices ginger root
} mix

8 slices cooked ham
4 Chinese black mushrooms,
　cut in half
1/2 T. soy sauce
1 T. melted chicken fat
　or sesame oil, or corn oil
10 1-inch pieces of green onion

❶ Scale and clean the fish. Diagonally make 4 cuts, 1 inch apart, on both sides of the fish. Rub mixture ① on the fish and inside the cuts. Place a slice of ham and Chinese black mushroom in the cuts as shown. Place the fish on a heatproof plate then pour the soy sauce and melted chicken fat on the fish.

❷ Bring water to a boil; steam the fish over high heat for 8 minutes. Remove the heatproof plate and drain the liquid from the plate (retain). Transfer the fish to a serving plate; sprinkle with green onion. Drizzle 1 T. boiling oil over the fish then pour the retained liquid over the fish. Serve.

Fig.1　Make 4 diagonal cuts through the meat to the bone.

Fig.2　Place a slice of ham and Chinese black mushroom in the slits.

清蒸海鮮　　Steamed Pomfret

①
1 whole pomfret (about 1 2/3 lbs.)
1 T. cooking wine or sherry
2 t. salt
2 slices ginger root
} mix

1/4 c. each: (shredded) pork tenderloin, Szechuan pickled mustard greens
2 T. shredded Chinese black mushroom
1 T. soy sauce
1/4 c. shredded green onions
dash of black pepper
3 T. oil

❶ Scale and clean the fish, if necessary. Rub the exterior and interior surface of the fish with mixture ①. Place the fish on a heatproof platter.

❷ Sprinkle the shredded pork, mustard greens, and Chinese black mushrooms on top of the fish. Sprinkle. 1 T. soy sauce on top. Put 1 cup of water in the wok; bring it to a boil. Place the heatproof platter, with the fish, in the wok. Steam over high heat for 10 to 15 minutes, or until the meat is just cooked. Remove the fish to a serving plate; retain the liquid from the heatproof platter. Sprinkle the shredded green onion and dash of black pepper on the fish. Place 3 T. oil in a hot wok. When the oil very hot, drizzle it over the fish. Drizzle the retained liquid on top of the fish.

■ Steaming time may vary due to size and thickness of fish. Use of gas or electric heat may cause a slight variation in cooking time.

Steamed Grouper

● Substitute grouper for pomfret; other ingredients and directions are the same.

■ Shredded green onion and coriander may be used as garnishes. Other garnishes may be used to taste.

豆豉蒸魚 Steamed Fish with Fermented Black Beans SERVES 12

	1 whole fish (about 1 2/3 lbs.)
	1 t. salt
①	1 T. cooking wine or sherry } mix
	dash of black pepper
	2 oz. pork tenderloin
	2 T. fermented black beans
②	1 T. each: chopped green onions, ginger root, garlic clove
	2 t. chopped hot red pepper
	1 T. soy sauce
	2 T. oil

❶ Scale and clean the fish, if necessary; pat dry. Rub the exterior and interior surface of the fish with mixture ①. Transfer the fish to a heatproof platter.

❷ Cut the pork tenderloin into cubes and sprinkle them on the fish. Sprinkle ② and soy sauce on top of the fish. Put 1 cup of water in the wok and bring to a boil. Place the heatproof platter, with the fish, in the wok and steam over high heat for 10 minutes, or until the fish is just cooked (do not overcook). Place 2 T. oil in the hot wok. When the oil is very hot, drizzle it over the fish. Steaming time may vary due to size and thickness of fish.

■ Use of gas or electric heat may also cause slight variation in cooking time. Any fresh fish may be used for this dish.

Fig.1 Rinse the fermented black beans.

Fig.2 Mix ②, meat, and soy sauce. Pour this mixture over the fish.

高麗魚條　Deep-fried Fish Strips

SERVES 6

2/3 lb. fish meat, cut
　　into 1/2-inch strips

① ⎰ 1/2 T. cooking wine or sherry
　　1/3 t. salt
　　1/2 egg white
　　1 T. cornstarch

3 egg whites

② ⎰ 2 T. cornstarch
　　2 T. flour
　　dash of salt

oil for frying
dash of Szechuan peppercorn salt

❶ Place the fish strips in a bowl and mix with ① . Beat the egg whites until stiff (about 5 minutes).Add ② to the egg whites to make a thick batter.

❷ Heat the wok then add oil. Separately dip each fish strip in the egg white batter then put into the wok. Deep-fry for about 3 minutes, or until the fish is cooked. Remove and drain. Serve; use Szechuan peppercorn salt for dipping.

■ Shrimp, chicken meat, beef, or pork may be used instead of fish.

■ To prepare Szechuan peppercorn salt, see p. 17.

Fig.1 Fold in ② to stiff egg whites to make a thick batter.

Fig.2 Coat the fish strips with the batter then deep-fry the fish.

番茄魚片　Fish Slices in Tomato Sauce

SERVES 6

2/3 lb. fish meat

① ┤
1/3 t. salt
1/2 T. cooking wine or sherry
1/2 egg white
1 T. cornstarch
1/2 c. oil for frying
1 each: small tomato ┐ cut into
small brown onion ┘ bite-size pieces

② ┤
3 T. ketchup
6 T. water, 1/2 T. sugar
1/2 t. each: salt, sesame oil
1 t. cornstarch
1/4 c. green peas, precooked

❶ Cut fish meat into 1/4-inch thick slices; mix with ① . Add 2 T. oil and mix before frying. The slices will separate easily during frying.

❷ Heat the wok then add 1/2 c. oil. Fry the fish slices until half cooked; remove the fish. Remove the oil from the wok. Reheat the wok then add 1 T. oil. Stir-fry the pieces of onion until fragrant. Add the tomato and stir. Add ingredients ② and fish slices; bring to a boil. Add green peas; stir to mix. Transfer to a serving plate; serve.

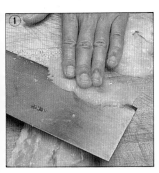

Fig.1　Slice the fish fillet.

Figs. 2, 3　Put the fish slices into hot frying oil. Remove when the fish turns white.

吉列魚排　　Deep-fried Fish Fillets

2/3 lb. fish fillets

① { 1 T. cooking wine or sherry
1/3 t. salt
dash of black pepper

② { 1/4 c. flour or cornstarch
1 egg, lightly beaten
1 c. grated bread crumbs

oil for frying

dash of Szechuan peppercorn salt
or ketchup, for dipping

❶ Place the blade of the cleaver parallel to the cutting surface then horizontally cut the fish meat into 1/2-inch slices. Mix the fish with ① ; set aside for later use. Place ② in separate plates.

❷ Coat the slices of fish with the cornstarch, egg, then bread crumbs (in order given).

❸ Heat the wok then add oil. Deep-fry the slices of fish over medium heat for 2 minutes, or until golden brown and the fish is cooked; remove and drain. Cut the fish fillets into 1-inch strips and arrange them on a platter. Serve with Szechuan peppercorn salt or ketchup.

■ To prepare Szechuan peppercorn salt, see p. 17.

Fig.1 Coat the fish with the flour then with the beaten egg.

Fig.2 Coat the fish with bread crumbs. Press the crumbs tightly with hand to prevent fish from breaking apart during frying.

翡翠斑球　　**Stir-fried Fish Balls with Broccoli**　　CANTONESE;
SERVES 6

①	2/3 lb. fish fillets 1/2 T. cooking wine or sherry 1/3 t. salt 1/2 egg white 1 T. cornstarch
	1/2 c. oil for frying 1 green onion, cut into 6 pieces 6 slices ginger root 1/2 lb. broccoli
②	3/4 t. each: salt, sugar dash of black pepper dash of sesame oil 3 T. water, 1 t. cornstarch

❶ Lightly score the fish fillet in a criss-cross patern. Cut the fillets into bite-size pieces. Separately add ① in the order given; mix after each addition. Before stir-frying, add 2 T. oil and mix so that the pieces of fish will separate easily during frying.

❷ Blanch the broccoli in boiling water; remove; drain and rinse in cold water (to cool); remove and drain.

❸ Heat the wok then add oil. Stir-fry the fish until it is cooked (this is precooking). Remove the fish then remove the oil from the wok. Reheat the wok and add 2 T. oil. Stir-fry the green onion, ginger root, and broccoli together. Add the fish and ②; turn heat to high; stir quickly to mix. Transfer to a serving plate and serve.

Fig.1　Lightly score the fish fillet in a crisscross pattern.

Fig.2　Cut the fillet into diagonal pieces.

韭黃炒鱔魚　Stir-fried Eels with Chives

SHANGHAI;
SERVES 6

1/2 lb. precooked eels
1/2 c. oil for frying
3 oz. yellow Chinese chives

① {
2 1/2 T. soy sauce
dash of sesame oil
1 t. sugar
3 T. water
1/2 T. cornstarch
}

② {
dash of black pepper
1 1/2 T. each: chopped green onion,
　　　　　　minced garlic clove
2 T. each: shredded ginger root,
　　　　　chopped coriander
}

❶ Cut the eels and yellow Chinese chives into 2 1/2-inch lengths.
❷ Heat the wok then add 1/2 c. oil. Deep-fry the eels over medium heat for 1 minute; remove and drain. Remove the oil from the wok. Reheat the wok then add 2 T. oil. Stir-fry the yellow Chinese chives; add the eel and ①. Turn the heat to high and stir quickly to mix. Transfer to a serving plate. Make a slight indentation in the center of the fried eels; place ② in the indentation. Heat the wok then add 2 T. oil; heat until very hot. Drizzle the hot oil over the green onion and garlic. Place coriander and shredded ginger root at both ends of the platter. Mix together before serving.

Fig.1 Remove any old leaves from the chives then wash them.

Fig.2 Cut the chives into 2-inch pieces.

塩酥蝦　　Stir-fried Salty and Crispy Shrimp

CANTONESE;
SERVES 6

2/3 lb. fresh shrimp, with shell

① { 1/4 egg, beat lightly
1/2 T. cornstarch

② { green onion
hot red pepper
garlic clove } chopped and combined to equal 2 T.

③ { 1/4 t. salt
dash of five-spice powder
dash of black pepper

❶ Rinse the shrimp and pat dry. Cut off the antennae and all appendages from the shrimp (still in shell). Devein and mix with ① ; let stand until ready for use.

❷ Heat the wok then add oil; deep-fry the shrimp for 1 1/2 minutes or until the shell is crispy; remove and drain. Remove the oil from the wok. Reheat the wok then add 1 T. oil. Stir-fry ② until fragrant. Add shrimp and ③ ; stir quickly to mix. Transfer to a serving plate and serve.

■ Five-spice powder is optional.

Fig.1　For family use, sprinkle ②and ③on the shrimp.

Fig.2　Shake the bowl to toss and mix the shrimp.

酥炸蝦　Deep-fried Crispy Shrimp

CANTONESE;
SERVES 12

① 24 medium-size fresh shrimp
1 T. cooking wine or sherry
1/3 t. salt

② 1 c. flour
1/2 t. baking powder
1 T. oil
3/4 c. water
oil for frying

❶ Shell the shrimp, leave tail intact. Devein and rinse; drain. Mix the shrimp with ① . Let stand until ready for use.

❷ Mix ingredients in ② in the following manner: Mix flour and baking powder together; add oil and water then mix to make a flour batter. If mixture is too dry, add water. (The batter should not be runny.)

❸ Heat the wok then add oil. *Hold the shrimp by the tail and dip it into the flour batter; put it in the oil*. Repeat between *for other shrimp. Deep-fry the shrimp for 2 minutes.or until they are cooked and the skins are crispy. Remove and drain. Transfer the shrimp to a serving plate. Serve with Szechuan peppercorn salt or ketchup for dipping.

■ To prepare Szechuan peppercorn salt, see p. 17.

Fig.1　Adjust the water measurement according to the dryness of the flour. Mix the flour and water to form a batter.

Fig.2　The batter is the right consistency when it coats the shrimp easily when dipped.

炸蝦丸   **Fried Shrimp Balls**   SERVES 12

① 2/3 lbs. raw shelled shrimp
1/2 t. salt
1 t. cooking w or sherry
dash of black pepper
1/2 t. sesame oil
1 egg white
1 T. cornstarch
1 oz. pork fat
oil for frying
dash of Szechuan peppercorn salt,
for dipping see p. 17.

❶ Rinse and devein the shrimp; drain. Use the side of the blade of a cleaver or a meat mallet to mash the shrimp. Chop the shrimp finely. Separately chop the pork fat finely. Mix chopped shrimp, pork fat, and ① in a bowl. Throw the mixture lightly against the inside of a mixing bowl to blend to a smooth paste (approximately 3 minutes).

❷ Heat the wok then add oil; turn off the heat after the oil is hot. *Take a portion of shrimp paste in palm of hand and squeeze hand to a fist so that the paste is forced out of the space between the thumb and index finger. Use a spoon, dipped in water to remove the formed ball. Put the shrimp ball in the oil. Repeat from* until all the mixture is used. Turn on the heat to medium; deep-fry the shrimp balls for about 3 minutes, or until they have expanded and are slightly golden. Remove, drain, and place on a serving plate. Serve with Szechuan peppercorn salt.

■ All shrimp balls may be coated with bread crumbs and set aside then deep-fried. If shrimp balls are not breaded, they must be deep-fried immediately.

Fig.1 To form shrimp paste: Mash the shrimp with a meat mallet or the flat side of a cleaver OR

Fig.2 Use a mixer to mash the shrimp. Add mixture ① and pork fat; mix to form a paste.

Fig.3 Take a portion of shrimp paste in the palm of hand. Flatten the paste with the thumb.

Fig.4 Squeeze hand to a fist so that the paste is forced out of the space between the thumb and index finger. Use a spoon, dipped in water, to remove the formed ball. (Dipping the spoon in water will prevent the shrimp paste from sticking to the spoon.)

鍋粑蝦仁　Stir-fried Shrimp over Crispy Rice

SZECHUAN;
SERVES 12

① 1/2 lb. raw, shelled shrimp
1 t. cooking wine or sherry
1/4 t. salt
1/3 egg white
3/4 T. cornstarch
3 c. oil for frying

② 3 T. ketchup, 1 T. sugar
3/4 t. salt, 3 c. water
1/4 c. green peas, precooked

③ 2 T. cornstarch ⎫ mix
2 T. water ⎭
5 oz. glutinous rice cakes

❶ Rinse and devein the shrimp; pat to dry. Separately add ① in order given; mix after each addition. Cut the rice cake into 1 1/2-inch squares.

❷ Heat the wok then add 2 T. oil. Add ② and bring to a boil. Add green peas and shrimp; cook over medium heat for 2 minutes. Add mixture ③ to thicken; stir. Add 1 T. oil and stir. Pour the shrimp mixture into a large bowl.

❸ Heat the wok then add oil. Deep-fry the rice cake squares until golden brown; remove and drain. Arrange the rice cake squares on a serving plate; pour shrimp mixture over rice cake squares; serve.

■ For a dramatic effect for dinner guests, pour the shrimp mixture over rice cakes at the table. The rice cakes and shrimp mixture combination create an impressive sound.

■ Gluttinous rice cake ("gwo ba") is a type of dry, puffed rice cake available in packages and is usually found in the oriental food section of food stores.

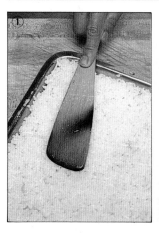

Fig.1 Crispy Rice: Place cooked rice on a cookie sheet; press tightly.

Fig.2 Bake the rice at warm until it is half-dried. Remove and cut the rice into pieces. Put the rice in the oven and bake until it is dry (about 24 hours).

五彩蝦仁 Stir-fried Shrimp with Assorted Vegetables   SERVES 6

① 1/2 lb. raw, shelled shrimp
1 t. cooking wine or sherry
1/4 t. salt
1/3 egg white
3/4 T. cornstarch
1/2 c. oil for frying

② 1/2 c. each: diced brown onion,
diced carrot
1/4 c. each: diced button
mushrooms, precooked
green peas

③ 1/3 t. salt, 1 t. cornstarch
dash of black pepper, sesame oil
2 T. water

❶ Rinse and devein shrimp; drain. Mix shrimp with ① in the order listed; mix after each addition. Before frying, add 1 T. oil and mix so that the shrimp will separate easily during frying.

❷ Heat the wok then add oil. Fry the shrimp over medium heat until cooked (precooking). Remove shrimp; remove oil from the wok. Reheat the wok then add 2 T. oil. Stir-fry the brown onions until fragrant. Add the remaining ingredients in ② add 2 T. water. Stir-fry until the liquid has almost completely evaporated and the ingredients are cooked. Add shrimp and ③; turn the heat to high; stir quickly to mix. Transfer to a serving plate and serve.

■ To save time, ingredients in ② may be precooked.

Fig.1 See. p. 116 to clean the shrimp. Cut the shrimp in half if it is large.

Fig.2 Mix the shrimp with wine, salt, and egg white; add cornstarch and mix.

青豆蝦仁　Stir-fried Shrimp with Green Peas

SERVES 6

① 1/2 lb. raw, shelled shrimp
1/4 t. salt
1 t. cooking wine or sherry
1/3 egg white
3/4 T. cornstarch
1/2 c. oil for frying
1 green onion, cut into 6 pieces
6 slices ginger root

② 1/3 t. each: cooking wine or sherry,
salt, sesame oil
dash of black pepper
1 t. cornstarch, 2 T. water
1 c. green peas, precooked

❶ Rinse and devein the shrimp; drain. Place the shrimp in bowl; add ① in order listed; mix after each addition. Before frying, add 1 T. oil and mix. The shrimp will separate easily during frying. Mix ② in a bowl; let stand for later use.

❷ Heat the wok then add oil. Fry the shrimp over medium heat until cooked (precooked). Remove the shrimp then remove the oil. Reheat the wok then add 1 T. oil. Stir-fry the green onion and ginger root until fragrant. Add the green peas; stir; add shrimp, and ② ; turn heat to high and quickly stir to mix. Transfer to a serving platter; serve.

Fig.1　Shell and devein the shrimp.

Fig.2　Mix the shrimp with salt and water. Rinse several times; drain. Add mixture ①(see p. 115, Fig. 2).

乾燒明蝦   **Spicy Stir-fried Prawns**

SZECHUAN;
SERVES 12

12 prawns (about 1 1/3 lbs.)
1 T. cornstarch
oil for frying

① {
2 T. chopped green onion
1 T. chopped ginger root
1/2 T. minced garlic clove
1 t. hot bean paste
1 T. fermented rice wine or
    cooking wine
4 T. ketchup

② {
3/4 t. salt, 1 T. sugar
1/2 T. cornstarch, 1 c. water

❶ Cut off the antennae and other appendages from the prawns; rinse and devein; drain. Before frying, coat the prawns with cornstarch.

❷ Heat the wok then add oil. Deep-fry the shrimp over high heat for 2 minutes,or until cooked; remove and drain Remove the oil from the wok. Reheat the wok then add 2T.oil. Stir-fry ① until fragrant. Add ② and bring to a boil; add shrimp and stir to mix. Transfer to a serving plate and serve.

■ If the prawns are small reduce the frying time.

Fig.1   Cut the back of the shrimp lengthwise; do not cut through.

Fig.2   Or the shrimp may be clipped with scissors before cooking; so it will be easier to eat.

鹹蜆   **Marinated Clams**   TAIWANESE; SERVES 6

2/3 lb. small fresh clams
1/2 c. soy sauce
5 garlic cloves, mashed
1 hot red pepper, sliced diagonally
① 1 t. white vinegar
1 t. sugar
3 T. cooking wine or sherry
2 T. cold boiled water

❶ Place the clams in an aluminum container with water to cover and let stand for 6 hours. (Clams will rid themselves of sand.)
❷ Clean the clams and put them in the aluminum container add water to cover. Place the container in a wok; put 1 cup of water in the wok. Cover and steam at low heat until the clams open to 1/6 inch. Remove the container of clams; drain. Transfer the clams to another deep bowl; add ① to marinate; refrigerate for 24 hours. Serve.
■ The steaming process allows the clams to open slightly; however, the meat is still uncooked. Clams may be pried open with a knife then placed in a deep bowl with ① and refrigerated for 24 hours.

Fig.1 Put water in a wok. Place the clams in a container then place the container in the wok. The temperature in the container will rise evenly so that the clams will open to the same size.

Fig.2 Pry open the clams with a knife.

全家福　　Ideal Family Stew　　SERVES 6

① {
1 T. each: chopped ginger root, green onion
6 chunky pieces each: sea cucumber, chicken meat
6 slices of cooked ham
6 ground pork balls
6 young bamboo shoots, canned
6 baby corns, canned
}

② {
1 1/2 c. water, 1/2 t. salt
1 T. cooking wine or sherry
}

③ {
2 1/2 T. soy sauce, 1/2 T. sugar
dash of black pepper, dash of sesame oil
}

④ {
6 slices of squid
1 small cucumber, cut lengthwise into 6 strips　(about 2 1/2 inches)
6 slices of carrot
}

⑤ {
1/2 T. cornstarch
1 T. water
} mix

- Heat the wok then add 4 T. oil. Stir-fry the green onions and ginger root. Separately add then stir ingredients in ① . Add ② ; bring to a boil. Turn heat to medium; cover and cook for 8 minutes. Add ③ and ④ ; bring to a boil again; add mixture ⑤ to thicken; stir. Transfer to a serving plate; serve.
- ■ This dish is very flexible. Ingredients in ① or ④ may be substituted with other ingredients such as fish balls, shrimp balls, bok choy, bamboo shoots, Chinese black mushrooms, and roast pork.
- ■ To prepare sea cucumber and squid, see p. 18.

Sea Cucumber with Brill Fish

1 1/3 lbs. sea cucumber,
　cut into pieces
1/6 lb. dried brill fish

① {
6 pieces green onion, 1 inch long
6 garlic cloves, mashed
6 slices bamboo shoot
6 Chinese black mushrooms
}

3 T. oil

② {
3 T. soy sauce
1 T. each: sugar, cooking wine, dash of black pepper
1/2 T. sesame oil
1 1/2 c. chicken stock
}

③ {
1 T. cornstarch
2 T. water
} mix

- Heat the wok then add 3 T. oil. Stir-fry ① ; add bamboo shoot and black mushrooms. Add ② and sea cucumber; cook over low heat for 5 minutes. Add the dried brill fish; cook until the sauce is reduced to half. Add mixture ③ ; stir and serve.

肉丸海參 **Pork Balls and Sea Cucumber** CANTONESE; SERVES 12

1 lb. sea cucumber
1/2 lb. ground pork

① {
1 t. cooking wine or sherry, 1/3 t. salt
dash of black pepper
2 T.water, 1 T. cornstarch
}

oil for frying
1 green onion, cut into 6 pieces
6 slices ginger root

② {
1 T. cooking wine or sherry
3 T. soy sauce
1/2 T. sugar,dash of black pepper
1/2 c. chicken stock
}

③ {
1/2 T. cornstarch
1 T. water
} mix

❶ Cut the sea cucumber into bite-size pieces.
❷ Mix the ground pork with ① . Heat the wok then add oil. Form the ground pork into balls and place them in the oil; deep-fry for 2 minutes, or until golden brown. Remove and drain. Remove the oil from the wok.
❸ Reheat the wok then add 3T. oil. Stir-fry the green onion and ginger root until fragrant. Add sea cucumber; stir; add ② and pork balls. Bring to a boil; cover to cook for 10 minutes, or until the liquid is reduced to 1/2 cùps. Add ③ to thicken liquid; stir. Transfer to a serving plate; serve.
■ To form ground pork into balls See P. 113, Figs. 1, 2, 3, 4.

Fig.1 Wash off all foreign matter from the sea cucumber and clean.

Fig.2 Cut the sea cucumber lengthwise into strips.

Fig.3 Cut the sea cucumber diagonally into pieces.

宮保魷魚 Stir-fried Squid with Dried Red Peppers

SZECHUAN;
SERVES 6

① 2 presoftened dried squid
　(about 2/3 lb.)
　3 dried red peppers, cut into pieces
　1 t. chopped garlic clove
　3 T. soy sauce
　1 T. sugar
　1/2 T. white vinegar
　1/2 T. sesame oil
　1 1/2 T. water
　2 t. cornstarch

❶ Rinse the squids and cut off the heads, tentacles, and tails, peel off the thin membrane from the surface of the squid. Cut each squid into 4 strips. Score the inside surface lengthwise and crosswise then cut it into bite-size pieces.

❷ Bring a pot of water to a boil; blanch the pieces of squid for 20 seconds, or until half cooked. When the pieces of squid curl up slightly, remove and drain them.

❸ Heat the wok then add 2T. oil, Stir-fry the dried red pepper until fragrant. Add chopped garlic and squid; stir to mix. Add ① and turn heat to high; mix quickly. Transfer to a serving platter; serve.

■ To presoften dried squid, see p. 18.

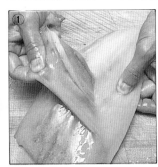

Fig.1 Remove the membrane from the squid.

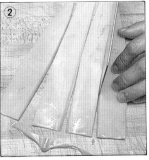

Fig.2 Cut the squid lengthwise into 4 strips.

Fig.3 Diagonally score the inside surface lengthwise.

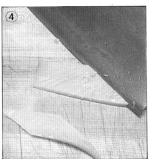

Fig.4 Diagonally score the inside surface crosswise then cut the strips into pieces.

生炒墨魚 Stir-fried Squid with Assorted Vegetables SERVES 6

2/3 lb. fresh squid

1 c. sliced celery ⎫
12 slices of carrot ⎭ precooked

① ⎧ 1 green onion, cut into 6 pieces
⎨ 6 slices of ginger root
⎩ 1/2 T. minced garlic clove

② ⎧ 1/3 t. salt
⎪ dash of black pepper
⎨ dash of sesame oil
⎪ 1 t. cornstarch
⎩ 1 1/2 T. water

❶ Cut off the heads, tentacles, and tails of the squids; remove the membrane and rinse. Score the inside surface lengthwise and crosswise; cut into bite-size pieces. (See P. 121, Figs. 1,2,3,4).

❷ Heat the wok then add 3 T. oil. Stir-fry ① until fragrant. Add the slices of celery and carrot; stir to mix. Add squid and stir until the pieces of squid curl. Add ② and mix quickly. Transfer to a serving plate and serve.

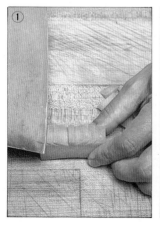

Fig.1 Carving the carrot:Cut the carrot into a rectangular shape. Diagonally cut slanted v-shaped strips on both sides of the carrot.

Fig.2 Slice the carrot lengthwise.

豆豉生蠔　Stir-fried Oysters with Fermented Black Beans

TAIWANESE;
SERVES 6

2/3 lb. oysters
1/2 t. salt

① {
1 T. minced ginger root
1 T. minced garlic clove
2 T. fermented black beans
}

1/2 c. chopped green onion

② {
2 1/2 T. soy sauce or oyster sauce
1 T. water
1 t. cornstarch
}

❶ Put the oysters in a bowl; add a dash of salt and mix. Rinse the oysters in fresh water. Blanch the oysters for 20 seconds in a pot of boiling water; remove and drain.

❷ Heat the wok then add 4 T. oil. Add ① and stir-fry until fragrant. Add oyster, green onion, and ②; turn heat to high; stir lightly and bring to a boil. Transfer to a serving plate; serve.

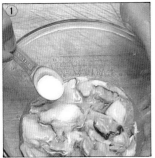  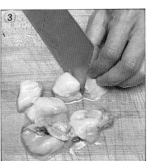

Fig.1　Put the oysters in a bowl; add 1/2 t. salt.
Fig.2　Mix the oysters and slat carefully. Rinse the oysters to remove the membrane and odd smell.
Fig.3　Halve the large oysters.

醬燒海蟹   Saucy Crabs

PEKING;
SERVES 6

1 1/3 lbs. soft-shelled crabs
cornstarch, for coating
oil for frying
1 green onion, cut into 6 pieces
6 slices ginger root

① {
1 1/2 T. sweet bean paste
1 T. each: cooking wine or
           sherry, soy sauce
1/2 T. sugar
1/2 c. water
} mix

dash of sesame oil

❶ Clean the crabs and cut them into pieces. Dip the open ends (meat) of the crabs into the cornstarch.
❷ Heat the wok then add oil. Fry the pieces of crab for 2 minutes, or until golden brown; remove and drain. Remove the oil from the wok.
❸ Reheat the wok then add 3 T. oil. Stir-fry the onion and ginger root until fragrant. Add ① and bring to a boil. Add the pieces of crab; stir to mix. Transfer to a serving plate; serve.

Fig.1 Method of Preparing a Crab (A)
       Cut the crab in half at belly.

Fig.2 Turn the crab over and open shelf of the crab; remove the gills.
       Clean off any foreign matter with a brush.

豉椒炒蟹   Stir-fried Crab with Bell Pepper

CANTONESE;
SERVES 6

1 1/3 lbs. soft-shell crabs
1/2 c. cornstarch
1 bell pepper, cut into bite-size
   pieces
oil for frying

① { green onion
   ginger root } chopped, combined
   garlic clove } to equal 1 1/2 T.
1 T. fermented black beans

② { 1 T. cooking wine or sherry
   3/4 t. each: salt, sugar
   1/2 c. water

❶ Rinse and drain the crabs. Cut them into small pieces then dip the open ends into cornstarch. This prevents the meat from falling out of the soft shell.

❷ Heat the wok then add oil. Fry the pieces of crab for 2 minutes, or until they are golden brown; remove and drain. Remove the oil from the wok. Reheat the wok then add 1T. oil. Add bell pepper and 1 T. water; stir until the bell pepper is soft; remove. Add 3 T. oil; stir-fry ① until fragrant. Add fried pieces of crab and ② ; cover and cook for 2-3 minutes; stir several times during cooking. When the crab is cooked and the liquid has reduced to almost dry, add the bell pepper; stir to mix. Transfer to a serving plate and serve.

Fig.3 Method of Preparing a Crab (B)
      Put the crab in boiling water until it stop moving; remove. Open the shelf of the crab and remove the gills. Clean off any foreign matter with a brush. Cut off the crab's legs then cut the crab into pieces.

Fig.4 Break the crab's claws with a mallet before using.

鮑魚草菇 Stir-fried Abalone with Straw Mushrooms CANTONESE;
SERVES 12

1 1-lb. can abalone (net 6 oz.)
2 c. straw mushrooms
12 stalks bok choy
1 green onion, cut into 6 pieces
6 slices ginger root

① {
1/2 T. cooking wine or sherry
1 c. stock
2 T. oyster sauce
1 T. soy sauce
dash of sesame oil
dash of sugar

② {
1 T. cornstarch
2 T. water
} mix

❶ Make 1/4-inch wide and 1/2-inch deep cuts across the abalone. Turn the abalone 45°(1/4 turn);then cut it into paper-thin slices. Remove any wilted leaves from the bok choy; cut it into 3-inch pieces. Boil half a pot of water. Separately blanch the bok choy and straw mushrooms for 3 minutes each.

❷ Heat the wok then add 3 T. oil; stir-fry the bok choy and add a dash of salt. Remove and arrange around the platter.

❸ Reheat the wok then add 3 T. oil. Stir-fry the onions and ginger root until fragrant. Stir-fry the mushrooms and add ① ; bring to a boil. Add mixture ② to thicken; stir. Add the abalone slices; stir to mix. Transfer to the center of the serving platter; serve.

■ Either fresh or canned straw mushrooms may be used for this dish.

Fig.1 Pour out the straw mushrooms and discard the liquid.

Fig.2 Halve the large mushrooms.

清燴鮑片 Braised Abalone with Assorted Vegetables SERVES 12

①
1 1-lb. can abalone (net 6 oz.)
6 tender bamboo shoots
6 baby corns
3 bok choy
3 Chinese black mushrooms
1 c. nappa cabbage, cut into bite-size pieces
1 green onion, cut into 6 pieces
6 slices ginger root

②
3/4 t. salt, 1 c. stock
dash of: sesame oil, black pepper, sugar

③
1 T. cornstarch
2 T. water
} mix

❶ Cut the abalone into paper-thin slices. Lengthwise, halve the bamboo shoots and baby corns. Cut the bok choy and Chinese black mushrooms into quarters.

❷ Heat the wok then add 3 T. oil. Stir-fry the green onion and ginger root until fragrant. Add ① ; stir briefly then add ② . Cover and cook to boiling; after it comes to a boil, cook for 2 more minutes. Add abalone slices and mixture ③ to thicken; stir. Transfer to a serving plate; serve.

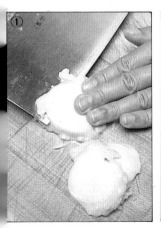

Fig.1 Slice the abalone diagonally.

Fig.2 Halve the bamboo shoots if they are too thick.

素雞　　Vegetarian Chicken Loaves　　SERVES 6

① 16 sheets bean curd skin
3 T. soy sauce
1 T. each:　sugar, sesame oil
1/3 t. salt
1 c. hot stock or hot water
2 16-inch squares cheese cloth

❶ Mix ① in a bowl; let stand for later use.

❷ Place a bean curd skin on a flat tray; *spread 1 T. of mixture ① on the skin. Place another bean curd sheet on top of mixture ①. Spread 1 T. of mixture on the skin*. Repeat from *6 times (each loaf takes 8 sheets). Fold in the sides to make an 8" by 2" oblong loaf; wrap the loaf in cheesecloth. Prepare another loaf with the remaining bean curd skins. Place the loaves in a steamer; steam for 15 minutes. Remove the loaves then remove the cheesecloth.

❸ Heat the wok then add 4 T. cooking oil or sesame oil. Fry the loaves on both sides over medium heat for about 30 seconds, or until both sides are medium brown. Remove and cut into 1-inch slices; arrange on a platter and serve.

■ The fried loaves may be cooked in soy sauce, if desired.

Fig.1　Place the bean curd skin on a cookie sheet. Spread 1 T. of mixture ① evenly on the skin of each layer.

Fig.2　Fold in the sides to make a 2-inch wide oblong loaf.

拌干絲　Bean Curd Noddle and Clery Salad　SERVES 6

4 oz. bean curd noodles
1/2 c. celery, cut into 2-inch strips
hot red pepper, shredded (to taste)
4 c. water
2 t. baking soda
① 1 t. salt
1 t. sesame oil

❶ Blanch the celery in boiling water; remove and plunge in cold water; remove and drain. Bring 4 c. water to a boil; add baking soda. When baking soda had dissolved, add noodles; stir with chopsticks to separate the noodles. Turn off the heat; let stand for 15 minutes. When the noodles become white (soft), remove and plunge them into cold water. Rinse several times to remove the baking soda solution.

❷ Mix the noodles, celery, hot red pepper, and ① together; serve.

■ Cooking time for the noodles will vary dependent upon the moisture in noodles. Test for doneness; noodles should not be overcooked because they disintegrate.

Bean Sprouts with Variety Colors

● See p. 166, "Stir-fried Shredded Chicken with Bean Sprouts", for ingredients and directions. Add green pepper, ham, shredded egg sheet, carrot, bamboo shoots, etc.

鑲豆腐   Stuffed Bean Curd

CANTONESE;
SERVES 6

1 pkg. bean curd
  (4 pieces to a package)
1 T. dried shrimp
1 oz. fish meat
2 oz. ground pork

① {
dash of salt
dash of cooking wine or sherry
1 T. water
1/2 T. cornstarch
}

② {
2 1/2 T. soy sauce
1/2 t. sugar
dash of black pepper
1 c. stock or water
}

③ {
1 t. cornstarch
2 T. water
} mix

❶ Soak the dried shrimp in water for 5-10 minutes; drain and chop finely with the fish meat. Add ground pork and ① ; mix thoroughly. This will be the filling.

❷ Diagonally cut each piece of bean curd to obtain 4 triangular pieces (to total 16 pieces). Stand the triangular pieces of bean curd so that 4 points are flat on working surface. *Hollow out the center for the filling. Do not remove too much bean curd because the sides will weaken. Sprinkle the cavity with cornstarch and stuff the cavity with some filling. Repeat from *for remaining 15 pieces of bean curd.

❸ Heat the wok then add 3T oil. Place the stuffed bean curd in the wok, filling side down. Fry over medium heat until golden brown. Add ② ; cover. Simmer until cooked. Add mixture ③ to thicken; stir. Sprinkle with sesame oil then transfer to a serving platter; serve.

■ The stuffed bean curd may be fried or steamed. Pieces may be triangular shaped or cut into 4 smaller squares.

Steamed Stuffed Bean Curd

Use the same ingredients as for "Stuffed Bean Curd" with the following exceptions: Use 1 pkg. soft bean curd (1 piece in a package) instead of 1 pkg. hard bean curd; 1/2 c. chicken stock instead of 1 c. chicken stock of mixture ② . For better results use soft bean curd for this dish.

❶ Cut the bean curd into 4 pieces. Hollow out the center slightly. Sprinkle the cavity with cornstarch and stuff it with some filling. To make filling, follow step ❶ of "Stuffed Bean Curd". Steam the bean curd for 8 minutes. Cut each piece into 4 pieces. Place the bean curd on a plate.

❷ Bring ② to a boil. Add mixture ③ to thicken; stir. Pour this mixture over the bean curd.

鍋塌豆腐　　Peking-style Fried Bean Curd

PEKING;
SERVES 6

1 pkg. bean curd (use 3 pieces)
1/2 c. flour
1 egg, beaten
1 T. each: green onion } chopped
          ginger root
① { 1 t. cooking wine or sherry
    1 t. salt
    1 t. sesame oil
    1/2 c. stock

❶ Cut the bean curd into 1/2-inch slices. Before frying, coat with flour then dip into the egg.

❷ Heat the wok then add 2 T. oil. Arrange the slices of bean curd evenly on the bottom of the wok. Fry over medium heat for about 1 minute, or until golden brown. Turn over, add 2 T. oil and fry until golden brown. Sprinkle with onion, ginger root, and ① . Pierce the bean curd with a fork to allow the liquid to seep through. Turn heat to low and cook until the liquid is absorbed by the bean curd.

■ Shrimp's eggs may be added to this dish if desired.

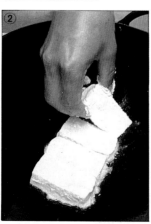

Fig.1 Cut the bean curd into 1/2-inch slices. Coat them with flour then dip them in the beaten egg.

Fig.2 Heat the wok. Arrange the slices of bean curd evenly on the bottom of the wok. Fry them until both sides are golden brown.

麻婆豆腐　Ma-Po's Bean Curd (Tofu)

① {
1 pkg. bean curd (use 3 pieces)
1 T. chopped green onion
1 t. each: (chopped) garlic clove,
　　　　ginger root
}

2 oz. ground pork
1 T. hot bean paste

② {
1 T. cooking wine or sherry
1 1/2 T. soy sauce
1 c. water, 1/2 t. salt
}

③ {
1 1/2 t. cornstarch
1 T. water
} mix

2 T. fresh garlic or green onion
　　(diagonally cut into pieces)
1/4 t. Szechuan peppercorn powder

❶ Cut the bean curd into 1/2-inch cubes.

❷ Heat the wok then add 3 T. oil. Stir-fry ① until fragrant; add ground pork and hot bean paste; stir to mix. Add ② and bean curd. Bring to a boil then turn heat to low; cook for 3 minutes.

❸ Add mixture ③ to thicken; stir. Sprinkle the pieces of garlic and Szechuan peppercorn powder over the bean curd. Transfer to a serving platter and serve.

■ Hot bean paste may be added, to taste. Szechuan peppercorn powder may be omitted.

■ If soft bean curd is used, reduce water in ② to 2/3 cups.

Bean Curd with Ground Pork

● See ingredients and directions for "Ma-Po's Bean Curd". Substitute hot bean paste with bean paste or soy sauce.

雞抓豆腐   "Gee Jua" Bean Curd   SERVES 6

① { 1 pkg. bean curd (4 pieces)
2 T. dry shrimps
4 T. Szechuan pickled
    mustard greens } chopped
1 T. each: green onion
    ginger root
2 oz. ground pork

② { 1 T. each: cooking wine or sherry,
    soy sauce
1/8 t. salt
1/3 c. water

③ { 1/2 T. cornstarch
1 T. water } mix

- Heat the wok then add 3 T. oil. Stir-fry ① until fragrant. Add the ground pork then stir-fry. Add the bean curd then stir-fry. Mash the bean curd. Add ② cook for 3 minutes. Add mixture ③ to thicken; stir. Transfer to a serving plate and serve.

Steamed Bean Curd with Ground Pork

☐1 { 1/2 lb. ground pork
2 pieces hard bean
    curd, mashed } mix
2 eggs

☐3 { 2 T. chopped green onions
1 1/2 T. soy sauce
1/2 T. sesame oil

☐2 { 1 T. cooking wine
1 t. each: salt,
    sesame oil
dash of black pepper
2 T. diced green
    onion
1/2 T. diced ginger
1 T. cornstarch } mix

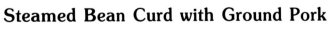

- Thoroughly mix mixture ☐1 and ☐2 together. Arrange the mixture evenly on a heatproof plate. Steam over high heat for 15 minutes; keep water boiling. Remove and sprinkle with ☐3. Serve.

千層豆腐　Deep-fried Layered Bean Curd

TAIWANESE;
SERVES 12

① { 3 oz. shelled shrimp, chopped finely
　　3 oz. ground pork

② { 1/4 t. each: salt, sugar, sesame oil
　　1 t. each: cooking wine or sherry,
　　　　　cornstarch
　　2 T. water, dash of black pepper

③ { bamboo shoot
　　carrot ⎫ chopped finely,
　　Chinese black ⎬ combined to
　　　mushroom ⎭ equal 1/4 c.
　　green onion

　　1 pkg. bean curd, 4 pieces

④ { 1 egg, 1/4 t. salt
　　1/2 c. flour, 4 T. water
　　oil for frying

❶ Mix①, ②, and③together in a bowl to make the filling. Divide the filling into 6 portions.

❷ Cut each square into 6 thin slices. To obtain stacks with 4 layers of bean curd each: put 1 slice of bean curd on a lightly greased platter; sprinkle with cornstarch and spread 1/3 of a portion of filling on the bean curd. Place another slice of bean curd on the filling. Continue to assemble layers until each stack has 4 layers.

❸ Mix④ to make a flour paste; separately dip each stack into the flour paste mixture.

❹ Heat the wok then add oil. If the wok is large all the stacks may be deep-fried together or fried in two batches. Deep-fry over medium heat for about 7 minutes, or until golden brown. Before removing, turn heat to high and fry for 1 minute. Remove and drain. Diagonally slice the bean curd stacks in half. Use soy sauce, oyster sauce, or ketchup as a dipping sauce. Serve.

■ Fewer layers may be assembled for family use.

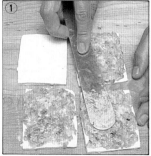

Fig.1 Spread a portion of filling on the slices of bean curd. Add a little water to make the spreading easier.

Fig.2 Stack the layers of bean curd on top of each other.

Fig.3 Use a spatula to lift the bean curd stacks. Spread mixture ④ over the bean curd then deep-fry them.

雙冬豆腐　Braised Chinese Mushrooms and Bean Curd

CANTONESE;
SERVES 6

1 pkg. bean curd (use 3 pieces)
oil for frying
2 green onions, cut into 12 pieces
6 slices ginger root
5 Chinese black mushrooms
1/2 c. slices of bamboo shoots
3 precooked bok choy, cut in half
　lengthwise

① { 1 c. stock, 2 1/2 T. soy sauce,
dash of black pepper, sesame oil

② { 1/2 T. cornstarch
1 T. water } mix

❶ Cut the bean curd into chunky, bite-size pieces; pat them dry. Heat the wok then add oil. Deep-fry the pieces of bean curd over high heat until golden brown. Remove and drain. Remove the oil from the wok.

❷ Reheat the wok then add 3 T. oil. Stir-fry the onion and ginger root until fragrant. Add Chinese black mushrooms and slices of bamboo shoot; stir to mix. Add ① and bean curd; bring to a boil. Cook for 3 minutes. Add bok choy; cook for 2 more minutes, or until the liquid is reduced to half. Add mixture ② to thicken. Transfer to a serving plate and serve.

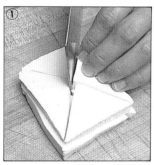

Fig.1 Cut the bean curd into three slices.

Fig.2 Lightly grease the strainer with oil and place the bean curd on the strainer.

Fig.3 Deep-fry the bean curd until it is golden brown.

香菇素腸　　Vegetable Mushroom Platter

① {
4 Su-Tsang (vegetarian rolls)
(about 2/3 lb.)
1/2 c. shredded Chinese black
mushrooms
2 T. shredded ginger root
1 T. soy sauce
1/3 t. salt
dash of black pepper
1 t. sesame oil

❶ Tear the su-tsang to shreds.
❷ Heat the wok then add 2 T. oil. Stir-fry the su-tsang for about 1 1/2 minutes. Move aside; add 1 T. oil; stir-fry Chinese black mushrooms until fragrant. Add the ginger root and ① ; return the su-tsang to the center of the wok; stir to mix. Transfer to a serving plate and serve.

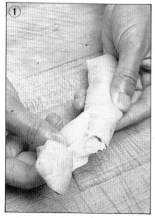 

Fig.1 Tear the su-tsang into strips.

Fig.2 Tear the su-tsang strips to shreds.

香菇烤麩 Stir-fried "Kau-fu" with Assorted Vegetables SERVES 6

① 4 pieces of kau-fu (2-inch squares)
oil for frying
1/4 c. each: Chinese black mushrooms; tiger lily
(tied into knots)
1/2 c. each: wood ears, bamboo
shoot slices
1 c. sliced pressed bean curd

② 1/2 T. each: cooking wine or sherry,
sesame oil
3 T. soy sauce, 1 T. sugar
dash of black pepper
dash of sesame oil
1 c. water

❶ Cut the kau-fu into 1/3-inch slices. Heat the wok then add oil. Deep-fry kau-fu until golden brown; remove and drain. Put kau-fu into a pot boiling water; cook for 3 minutes. Remove and squeeze the kau-fu to remove excess water.

❷ Place the kau-fu, ①, and ② in a deep pot; bring to a boil. Cover and turn heat to low; cook for 8 minutes. Remove to a serving plate; serve.

■ "Kau-fu" is a spongy-type of ingredient made from wheat gluten that may be stored for a long time. It may be found in the refrigerated section of markets, where bean curd is found.

Fig.1 Slice the kau-fu.

Fig.2 Deep-fry the kau-fu until it is golden brown.

羅漢素菜 Stir-fried Vegetarian Platter

CANTONESE;
SERVES 6

① 1 1/2 oz. bean curd stick ("fu dzu")
20 fried gluten balls ("mien jin pau")
3 stalks bok choy
1/4 c. Chinese black mushrooms
6 slices each: precooked bamboo
shoot, carrot
1/2 c. wood ears
1 vegetarian roll ("su tsang"), sliced

② 1 t. each: cooking wine or sherry,
sugar, white vinegar
3 T. soy sauce, 1 c. water
dash of black pepper, sesame oil

③ 1 t. cornstarch ⎫ mix
1 T. water ⎭

❶ Break the bean curd stick into several pieces. Heat the wok then add oil; deep-fry bean curd over medium heat for 20 seconds, or until pieces of been curd stick expand. Remove and drain. Put 3 c. water and 1 T. baking soda into a pot. Put the bean curd stick into the pot; cook over medium heat for 10 minutes, or until soft. Remove and rinse to remove the baking soda solution. Cook gluten balls in boiling water to remove the oil; remove and drain. Lengthwise, cut each stalk of bok choy into 4 pieces; blanch in boiling water. Remove and plunge them into cold water; remove and drain.

❷ Place the bean curd stick, gluten balls, ① and ② in a deep pot; bring to a boil; cover and turn heat to low. Cook for 8 minutes; add the bok choy; cook for another 2 minutes. Add mixture ③ to thicken; stir; transfer to a serving plate; serve.

Fig.1 Break the bean curd stick into several pieces.

Fig.2 Deep-fry the bean curd for 1 minute or until the bean curd sticks expand; remove.

三鮮百頁   **Stuffed Bean Curd Rolls**   SERVES 6

8 bean curd sheets ("bai ye")

① { 1 t. baking soda / 2 c. water } mix

② { 2 oz. shelled shrimp, chopped finely / 3 oz. ground pork, 1/4 t.salt / dash of sesame oil

③ { liquid (retained from bean curd rolls) / stock } together to equal 3/4 cups / 1/4 c. each: Chinese black mushrooms, bamboo shoots } shredded / 1/4 t. salt

④ { 1 t. cornstarch / 2 t. water } mix / 1 t. sesame oil

❶ Soak the bean curd sheets in mixture ① for 20 minutes. Rinse several times to remove the baking soda solution. Set aside for later use.

❷ Mix ② together to make the filling; divide into 8 portions. *Place one portion of filling diagonally across one bean curd sheet; fold bean curd sheet to enclose the filling and to form a roll. Repeat from *7 times. Place the rolls on a heat-proof plate. Place the plate in a steamer; steam over high heat for 10 minutes. Remove the rolls and retain the liquid (add to ③). Cut each roll in half; arrange on serving plate.

❸ Place ③ in a pot and bring the liquid to a boil; add mixture ④ to thicken; stir; add 1 t. sesame oil. Pour the mixture over the bean curd rolls; serve.

Fig. 1 Soak the bean curd sheets in mixture① until soft.

Fig. 2 Remove and rense them several times to remove the baking soda solution.

八寶辣醬　Eight Treasure Stir-fried Vegetables

PEKING;
SERVES 6

1/4 c. each: raw, shelled peanuts and green soy beans
1/4 c. each: diced, canned bamboo shoots, carrots, cucumber
1/2 c. each: diced pork tenderloin, diced pressed bean curd

① ⎰ 1 t. cornstarch
　 ⎱ 1/2 T. cooking wine or sherry

② ⎧ 1 t. hot bean paste
　 ⎨ 1 T. each: sweet bean paste, soy sauce
　 ⎩ 1/2 T. sugar

❶ Cook peanuts, soy beans, and carrots separately in water. Mix pork with ① ; set aside for later use. Mix ② in a bowl and set aside for later use.
❷ Heat the wok then add 3 T. oil. Stir-fry the meat until cooked; add peanuts and all other ingredients; stir to mix; add ② ; stir for 2 minutes. Transfer to a serving plate and serve.
■ This dish is very adaptable—ingredients may be varied to taste.

Stir-fried Chicken with Green Onion

2/3 lb. chicken, cut into 1/2 inch cubes)

1 ⎧ 1/2 T. cooking wine
　 ⎨ 1 T. each: soy sauce, cornstarch
　 ⎩ 1/2 c. oil

1 green onion, cut into 6 pieces
1/2 c. diced green pepper
1/2 c. diced bamboo shoots

2 ⎰ same as mixture ② of "Eight Treasure Stir-fried
　 ⎱ Vegetables"

❶ Mix the chicken with 1 . Heat the wok then add oil; stir-fry the chicken meat until it is cooked. Remove.
❷ Heat the wok then add 2 T. oil. Stir-fry the green onion, green pepper, and bamboo shoots. Add 2 and chicken; mix well.

螞蟻上樹 Stir-fried Bean Threads with Ground Pork

SZECHUAN;
SERVES 6

3 oz. ground pork
2 pkg. bean threads (3 oz.)

① { 2 T. chopped green onions
1/2 T. chopped ginger root
1/2 T. hot bean paste

② { 2 T. soy sauce
3/4 t. salt
1 t. sugar
2 c. stock or water

❶ Soak the bean threads in water until soft; remove and drain. Make several cuts through the bean threads to shorten the lengths.

❷ Heat the wok then add 3 T. oil. Stir-fry the pork for about 2 minutes; add ① ; stir to mix. Add ② and bean threads; bring to a boil. Turn heat to low and cook for 2-3 minutes, or until the liquid has almost completely evaporated. Remove and serve. Chopped green onions may be sprinkled on top of the bean threads.

Fig.1 Stir-fry the ground pork. Add①; stir to mix.

Fig.2 Add ② and bean threads.

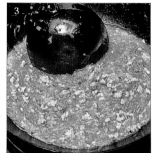

Fig.3 After boiling, turn heat to low and cook for a few minutes or until the liquid has almost completely evaporated.

141

三色蛋　　　Three-color Egg Slices

3 salty eggs
3 "thousand year old" eggs
3 eggs
① { 1/2 t. salt
1 T. lard or sesame oil
3 T. water

❶ Cook the salty eggs in boiling water until hard boiled. Shell and dice them into 1/2-inch cubes. Dice the thousand year old eggs into 1/2-inch cubes.

❷ Beat the chicken eggs then mix them with ① ; add the diced eggs; mix. Lightly oil a 6"x4" mold or box; pour the egg mixture into the mold then place it in a steamer. Steam over medium heat for 20 minutes, or until the eggs are firm; remove the mold from the steamer and let cool. Invert the mold to remove the steamed eggs. Slice and arrange them on a serving plate; serve.

■ A lightly oiled piece of heavy-duty cellophane may be used to line the greased mold for easy removal of egg mold.

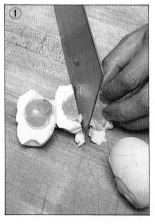 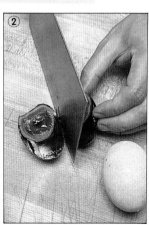

Fig.1 Cook the salty eggs in boiling water until they are hard; shell and dice them.

Fig.2 Shell and dice the thousand year old eggs. Mix the salty eggs the thousand year old eggs, eggs and ① together.

142

蛋餃子 Golden Egg Dumplings

PEKING;
SERVES 6

①	4 oz. ground pork pinch of salt 1 t. cooking wine or sherry dash of black pepper, sesame oil 1 1/2 T. water 1/2 T. cornstarch
	4 eggs
②	1/2 T. cornstarch 1/2 T. water } mix
③	1 c. stock or water 1 T. soy sauce 1/2 T. cooking wine or sherry 1/4 t. salt, dash of sugar

❶ Mix the ground pork with ① to make the filling. Lightly beat the eggs; add mixture ② and mix. Set aside for later use.

❷ Heat the wok then turn the heat to low. Lightly oil the wok. Spoon 1 T. egg mixture into the wok and rotate the wok to form a 2 1/2 inch pancake; place 1 t. filling in the middle and fold the egg pancake over in half. Cook over low heat; cook both sides until golden; remove. Repeat this step to make 12-15 dumplings.

❸ Put ③ and egg dumplings in a pot; cover and cook over medium heat until the filling is cooked and the liquid has almost evaporated; remove. Transfer to a serving plate.

Fig.1 A ladle can be used to form the egg dumplings. Spoon 1 T. egg mixture into the ladle and rotate the ladle to form a 2 1/2 inch pancake. Place 1 t. filling in the middle.

Fig.2 Fold the egg pancake over in half.

番茄炒蛋　Stir-fried Eggs with Tomato

SERVES 6

① 5 eggs
1/4 t. salt
dash of black pepper
1 green onion, chopped finely
1 tomato, diced

② pinch of salt
1/2 t. sugar
1 T. each: ketchup, water
1 t. cornstarch

❶ Add ① to eggs and beat lightly; add the green onion and mix.
❷ Heat the wok then add 2 T. oil; stir-fry the tomato then add ②. Stir briefly while the liquid thickens; remove. Clean the wok.
❸ Reheat the wok then add 5 T. oil. Hold the wok and rotate it to swirl the oil around the lower two-thirds of the wok. Turn the heat to high. Pour in the egg mixture and stir-fry until it becomes slightly firm; add the tomato liquid from step ②. Stir quickly to mix, do not overcook. Immediately transfer to a serving plate; serve.

Scrambled Eggs with Dried White Radish

① 4 eggs
1/4 t. salt
dash of black pepper

1/2 c. dried white radish, diced
1/4 c. chopped green onions
4 T. oil

❶ Beat the eggs and ① together. Add the dried white radish and green onions.
❷ Heat the wok then add 4 T. oil. Pour in the egg mixture and cook until the mixture is set. Press the egg mixture with a spatula to form a pancake-like shape. Rotate the wok to maintain even heat and browning. Cook until both sides are golden brown. If the eggs are too dry, add oil while the eggs are frying.

士司鵪蛋   **Shrimp Toast with Quail Eggs**   SERVES 12

8 quail eggs
5 slices white bread
1/2 lb. raw, shelled shrimp

① {
1 t. cooking wine or sherry
1/4 t. salt
1/2 egg white
1 T. cornstarch
}

1 T. each: chopped ham,
           black sesame seeds
15 sprigs of coriander (cilantro)
oil for frying

❶ Hard boil the eggs; shell and cut each in half lengthwise. Cut off the bread crusts then cut each slices into thirds; trim each third to form a diamond-shaped piece.

❷ Rinse and devein the shrimp; pat to dry. Mash the shrimp with a meat mallet. Put the mashed shrimp in a bowl; add ① and mix to make a paste (about 3 minutes). Divide the mixture into 15 portions.

❸ *Spread 1 portion of shrimp paste on a piece of bread; place an half egg, curve side up, on the shrimp paste. Add a little more shrimp paste around edges of egg to secure it in place and to smooth the surface. Dip the tip of a chopstick in chopped ham to pick up ham then place the ham on the shrimp paste. Repeat the dipping chopstick process for sesame seeds. Place one sprig of coriander on the shrimp paste. Repeat from *for the remaining pieces of bread.

❹ Heat the wok then add oil; deep-fry the shrimp paste bread slices over medium heat for about 2 minutes, or until golden brown. Remove, drain, and place on a serving plate; serve.

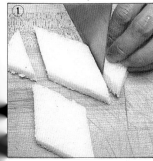

Fig.1 Cut the white bread into diamond-shaped pieces.

Fig.2 Spread one portion of shrimp paste on a piece of bread. Place half of an egg, curve side up, on the shrimp .

Fig.3 Smooth the surface of the shrimp paste. Place a sprig of coriander, a few black sesame seeds, and bits of ham on the shrimp paste for decoration.

洋菇鵪蛋　Braised Mushrooms with Quail Eggs

CANTONESE;
SERVES 12

24 quail eggs
2 T. soy sauce
2 c. oil for frying
1 green onion, cnt into 6 pieces
2 c. canned button mushrooms

① {
1/2 T. cooking wine or sherry
2 T. soy sauce
1/4 t. salt
1/2 t. saugar
dash of black pepper
1 c. stock
}

② {
1 T. cornstarch
1 T. water
} mix

3 bok choy

❶ Hard boil the quail eggs; remove. Shell and mix with 2 T. soy sauce. Set aside for later use.

❷ Heat the wok then add oil; deep-fry the quail eggs until golden brown; remove and drain. Remove the oil from the wok. Reheat the wok; add 3 T. oil. Stir-fry the onions until fragrant; add button mushrooms; stir. Add ① and cook for 2 minutes; add quail eggs. Add mixture ② to thicken; stir. Arrange cooked vegetable on a serving plate. Place the mushrooms and the eggs on the vegetable.

■ To prepare cooked vegetable, see p. 67, Figs. 1, 2.

Fig.1 Boil the quail eggs until hard. Remove and shell.

Fig.2 Mix with soy sauce while eggs are still hot.

Fig.3 Deep-fry the eggs until they are golden brown.

鹹蛋蒸肉　Steamed Salty Eggs with Meat

CANTONESE;
SERVES 6

① 2 salty egg yolks
2/3 lb. ground pork
1/2 T. cooking wine or sherry
1/2 t. salt
dash of sesame oil
1/2 T. cornstarch
1 salty egg white
1 t. chopped garlic clove
1 salty egg white

❶ Cut each yolk in half lengthwise then pat to shape thin round patties.

❷ Thoroughly mix the pork with ① . Shape the mixture into a patty 7 1/2 inches in diameter. The center should be thinner than the outer edges; slightly concave shape. (It is more convenient to form this meat patty on a heatproof plate.) Arrange the egg yolk patties on the meat patty. Pour the egg white on the egg yolks and meat. Place in a steamer and steam for 20 minutes over high heat, or until cooked. Remove and serve.

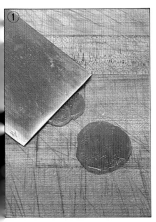
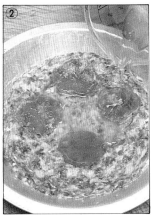

Fig.1 Separate the egg white and egg yolk of the salty eggs. Cut the egg yolks in half lengthwise then pat them to shape thin round patties.

Fig.2 Shape the pork mixture into a slightly concave-shaped patty. Arrange the egg yolk patties on the meat patty. Pour the egg white on the egg yolk and meat.

147

東坡綉球　　　Shredded Egg Balls

	3 eggs, for egg sheet (see p. 20)
①	4 oz. ground pork 2 oz. raw, shelled shrimp, chopped finely 2 shredded Chinese balck mushrooms
②	1/2 T. cooking wine or sherry 1/3 t. salt, dash of black pepper 1/2 t.sesame oil 1 T. each: cornstarch, water
③	1/2 c. stock pinch of salt
④	1 t. cornstarch 1 1/2 t. water } mix

❶ Shred the egg sheets.

❷ Mix ingredients ① with ② to make the filling; divide the filling into 12 portions. *Form each portion into a ball. Coat a meat ball with the shredded egg sheet . Repeat from* 11 times. Oil a heatproof plate. Place the shredded egg sheet balls on the plate; steam over high heat for 6 minutes.Remove the plate and transfer the shredded egg sheet balls to a serving plate.

❸ Place ③ in a sauce pan; bring to a boil. Add mixture ④ to thicken; stir. Pour this mixture over the steamed shredded egg balls. Serve or garnish serving plate with cooked vegetables.

■To make egg sheet See P. 79, Figs. 1, 2, 3.

Fig.1 To make egg ball:Place the shredded egg sheets on a plate. Shape the filling into 12 balls.(See p. 113, Fig. 4 for shaping balls.)

Fig.2 Coat the meat balls with shredded egg sheets.

搶白菜 Stir-fried Cabbage with Szechuan Peppers

SZECHUAN;
SERVES 6

① { 1 lb. cabbage or nappa cabbage
3 dried hot red peppers
1 t. Szechuan peppercorn
1/2 T. mashed ginger root

② { 1/2 T. each: cooking wine or sherry,
white vinegar, sugar
1/2 T. sesame oil
3/4 T. soy sauce
1/3 t. salt
1/2 t. cornstarch

❶ Rinse the cabbage and cut it into 2-inch squares. Cut the dried hot red peppers into 1-inch pieces.

❷ Heat the wok then add 3 T. oil. Add the cabbage and 3 T. water; turn the heat to high and stir-fry until the cabbage is soft but crunchy, do not overcook. Remove and drain water.

❸ Reheat the wok then add 2 T. oil. Stir-fry ① until fragrant; remove and discard ①. Return the cabbage and ② to the wok; stir to mix. Transfer to a serving plate and serve.

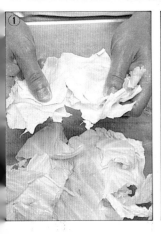

Fig.1 Tear or cut the cabbage into 2-inch squares.

Fig.2 Diagonally cut the dried hot red peppers into 1-inch pieces; remove the seeds

鑲青椒   Stuffed Bell Peppers

4 bell peppers
1/2 lb. ground pork
2 oz. raw, shelled shrimp
1 1/2 T. dried shrimp

① 1/2 T. cooking wine or sherry
1/3 t. salt
2 1/2 T. water
1 T. cornstarch

② 2 T. fermented black beans
1/2 T. minced garlic clove
1/2 T. chopped ginger root

③ 1 T. soy sauce, 1 c. water
dash of sugar

❶ Clean and devein shrimp; pat dry. Soak the dried shrimp in water until softened. Chop all shrimp finely; mix with ground pork and add ① to make filling. Divide filling into 12 portions.

❷ Cut each bell pepper into thirds; remove seeds. Trim each piece to a 2 1/2-inch circle; sprinkle cornstarch on the inside of the peppers. *Put one portion of filling on the circle of bell pepper; smooth the surface with a spoon. Repeat from* 11 times.

❸ Heat the wok then add 3 T. oil. Place the stuffed peppers in the wok, meat side down. Fry for 1 minute, or until golden brown; remove. Reheat the wok then add 2 T. oil. Stir-fry ② until fragrant; add the stuffed peppers and ③. Cover and cook over medium heat for 8 minutes, or until the liquid has reduced to 1/3 cup. Remove to a serving plate and serve.

Fig.1 Cut 3 or 4 round shapes from the large bell peppers. Cut the small bell peppers in half.

Fig.2 Sprinkle a little cornstarch on the inside surface of the peppers. Put one portion of filling on the bell peppers; smooth the surface with a spoon or spatula.

鑲苦瓜 Stuffed Bitter Squash with Fermented Black Beans

TAIWANESE;
SERVES 6

2/3 lb. bitter squash
1/2 lb. ground pork

① {
1/3 t. salt
1 t. minced garlic clove
dash of sesame oil
1/2 T. cornstarch

1 hot red pepper
1 T. fermented black beans

② {
1/3 t. salt
1/2 t. sugar
1 c. water

❶ Cut off the ends of the squash then cut them into slices 1/3 inch thick. Remove and discard the seeds. Bring 1/2 pot of water to a boil; add 1/2 t. salt and the sliced squash. Cook for 2 minutes. Remove the slices of squash then plunge them into cold water to cool; remove and drain. Shred the hot red pepper.

❷ Mix the ground pork with ① to make the filling.

❸ Lightly sprinkle cornstarch in the cavities of the squash then stuff them with filling.

❹ Heat the wok then add 3 T. oil. Fry the stuffed squash on both sides until the meat is golden brown; remove. Reheat the wok then add 2 T. oil; stir-fry the fermented black beans and hot red pepper until fragrant. Add the squash and ②. Cover and cook over medium heat for 8 minutes, or until the liquid is reduced to 1/3 cup. Transfer to a serving plate; serve.

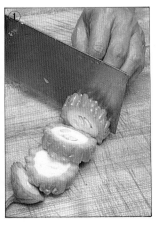
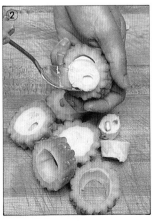

Fig.1 Cut off the ends of the squash. Cut the squash into slices 1/3 inch thick.

Fig.2 Remove and discard the seeds of the squash.

鑲百花菇 Stuffed Mushrooms with Shrimp Paste

CANTONESE;
SERVES 12

① {
24 small Chinese black mushrooms
1 green onion, cut into 6 pieces
1 slice ginger root
dash of cooking wine or sherry
1/4 t. each: salt,sugar
2 T. water, 1/2 T. soy sauce
2/3 lb. raw, shelled shrimp
1 oz. pork fat

② {
1 t. cooking wine or sherry
1/2 t. salt, 1 egg white, 1 T. cornstarch
dash of black pepper, sesame oil
1 T. chopped ham
24 leaves of coriander (cilantro)

③ {
1/4 t. each: salt, sesame oil
1/2 c. stock, 3/4 t. cornstarch
12 stalks, precooked Chinese broccoli

❶ Soak the mushrooms in water; drain and remove stems (discard). Mix ① with mushroom caps and steam over medium heat for 20 minutes; remove and drain.

❷ Rinse and devein the shrimp; drain and chop finely with the pork fat. Place the mixture in a bowl and add ②; stir to make a paste (about 3 minutes). Divide mixture into 24 portions.

❸ *Sprinkle cornstarch on the light side of the mushroom cap. Use a spoon to spread a portion of filling over the surface and to make it smooth. Place 1 leaf of coriander on the shrimp paste; sprinkle with the chopped ham. Repeat from *for remaining portions. Place the stuffed mushrooms on a lightly oiled heatproof plate; steam over high heat for 6 minutes. Remove.

❹ Heat the wok then add 3 T. oil. Add the Chinese broccoli, dash of salt and cooking wine; stir until vegetables are hot. Remove and drain. Place on a serving plate; garnish with the vegetable. Place the mushrooms in the center of the plate. Bring ③ to a boil; pour over the mushrooms and serve.

Fig.1 To make the surface of the shrimp paste smoother, add a little water before smoothing the surface.

Fig.2 Garnish with a sprig of coriander and a little chopped ham

蟹肉草菇 Stir-fried Crab Meat with Straw Mushrooms   SERVES 6

1 crab (about 1 lb.)
① {
2 green onions
2 slices ginger root
1/2 T. cooking wine or sherry
}
2 c. canned straw mushrooms
1 green onion, cut into 6 pieces
6 slices ginger root
② {
1 t. cooking wine or sherry
1/2 t. salt, 1 c. stock
dash of black pepper, sesame oil
}
③ {
1 1/2 T. cornstarch
2 T. water
} mix
14 stalks bok choy

❶ Clean the crab. Steam it with ① over high heat for 15 minutes. Remove the meat from the shell. (One-half cup canned crab meat may be used.) Set aside. Blanch the bok choy in boiling water, remove, drain, and plunge into cold water to cool. Remove and drain.

❷ Heat the wok then add 2 T. oil. Stir-fry the pieces of onion and ginger root until fragrant. Add mushrooms; stir and add ②. Bring to a boil. Add the crab meat, and mixture ③ to thicken; stir. Remove to a serving plate.

❸ Reheat the wok then add 3 T. oil. Add bok choy and a dash of salt; stir until vegetables are hot. Remove and drain; arrange around the rim of the plate. Transfer the crab meat and mushroom mixture to the center of the serving plate; serve.

■ See P. 67, Figs. 1, 2 to prepare bok choy.

Fig.1   Arrange the bok choy, curve side up, by overlapping it around the rim of the plate. Place the remaining bok choy in the center.

Fig.2   OR arrange the bok choy, cut side up, around the rim of the plate.

香菇菜心　Stir-fried Mushrooms and Bok Choy

1 1/3 lbs. bok choy
12 small Chinese black mushrooms
1 green onion, cut into 6 pieces

① {
1/2 T. cooking wine or sherry
3/4 t. salt
dash of black pepper
dash of sesame oil
1 1/2 c. stock or water
}

② {
1 1/2 T. cornstarch
2 T. water
} mix

❶ Remove any wilted leaves from the bok choy; halve or quarter each stalk lengthwise, depending on the thickness. Blanch in boiling water remove and plunge into cold water. When cool, remove and drain. Soak the black mushrooms in water; remove, drain, and cut off the stem (discard stems).

❷ Heat the wok then add 3 T. oil. Stir-fry the green onions until fragrant Add the black mushrooms and bok choy; stir. Add ①, cook over medium heat for 3 minutes. Arrange the bok choy stalks around the plate, leafy ends toward the center. Put the black mushrooms in the center. Add mixture ② to thicken; stir and serve.

■ Spinach may be substituted for the bok choy. (See P. 67, Figs. 1, 2 ② to prepare bok choy)

■ The bok choy may be arranged around the rim of the plate to encircle the mushroom.

● Family (simple) style for ②: Do not separate the mushrooms and bok choy, just add mixture ②, stir and serve.

扒金銀菇 Gold And Sliver Mushrooms

12 small Chinese black mushrooms

① {
1 1/2 T. soy sauce
1 T. oil
dash of cooking wine or sherry
dash of sugar
1/2 c. stock
}

2 lbs. bok choy
1 c. button mushrooms

② {
1/2 t. salt
1/2 c. stock
}

③ {
1 T. cornstarch
2 T. water
} mix

1/4 c. evaporated milk

❶ Soak the Chinese black mushrooms in water; remove; drain and steam with ① for 20 minutes. Blanch the button mushroom in boiling water. Remove and drain. Cut each bok choy in half lengthwise. Blanch in boiling water; remove and plunge into cold water. When cool, remove and drain.

❷ Heat the wok then add 2 T. oil. Add bok choy and a dash of salt; stir until bok choy is hot; remove. Arrange the bok choy around the rim of a serving plate.

❸ Bring the steamed black mushrooms with broth to a boil. Add 1/2 of mixture ③ to thicken; stir. Transfer to one side of the serving plate. Put button mushrooms with ②; bring to a boil. Add remaining half of mixture ③ to thicken; stir. Add milk and stir. Place on the opposite side of the black mushrooms and serve.

■ See P. 67, Figs. 1, 2 to prepare bok choy.

Stir-fried Bean Sprouts with Vinegar

1/2 lb. bean sprouts, remove the ends

1/4 c. shredeed bell pepper

1/2 t. Szechuan peppercorn

3 T. oil

① {
3/4 t. salt
1 t. sugar
1 T. vinegar
}

● Heat the wok then add 3 T. oil. Stir-fry the Szechuan peppercorns until fragrant; remove. Stir-fry the bean sprouts, shredded bell pepper, and ①. Remove and serve.

醬燒冬筍　Saucy Stir-fried Bamboo Shoots

SZECHUAN;
SERVES 6

3 c. precooked bamboo shoots
(about 2/3 lb.), cut into
bite-size pieces

① {
2 T. sweet bean paste
2 T. soy sauce
1 T. sugar
1/2 T. cooking wine or
sherry
} mix

1/2 c. water
1 T. sesame oil
1/2 lb. green leafy vegetable

❶ Heat the wok then add 3 T. oil. Stir-fry the bamboo shoots over medium heat for 2 minutes. Add mixture ① ; stir to mix. Add water and cook for 5 minutes, or until the liquid has almost completely evaporated. Add 1 T. Sesame oil. Transfer to a serving plate.

❷ Clean the wok then reheat it. Place 2 T. oil in the wok. Stir-fry the green leafy vegetable; add a dash of salt. Remove and drain. Arrange the vegetable on both sides of the bamboo shoots, as shown. Serve.

Saucy Stir-fried Eggplant

1 1/3 lbs. Chinese eggplant
oil

3 T. chopped garlic
1/2 T. chopped ginger root

① {
Use the same ingredients as
in ① of "Saucy Stir-fried
Bamboo Shoots"
}

❶ Cut the eggplants into long pieces. Deep-fry them until soft.
❷ Heat the wok then add 2 T. oil. Stir-fry the green onion and ginger root. Add ① and stir. Add 1/4 c. water and the eggplant; cook for 3 minutes or until the liquid has almost evaporated.

蠔油雙冬

Stir-fried Mushrooms and Bamboo Shoots with Oyster Sauce

CANTONESE;
SERVES 6

1 c. Chinese black mushrooms
1 1/2 c. bamboo shoots,
    cut into bite-size pieces
1 c. oil for frying

① 2 T. oyster sauce
1 T. soy sauce
1 t. sugar
1 1/2 c. water
dash of sesame oil

② 1/2 T. cornstarch
1 T. water } mix

6 bok choy or broccoli
(flowerets for garnish)

❶Cut each bok choy in half lengthwise and blanch in boiling water. Remove and plunge into cold water. When cool, remove and drain.

❷Heat the wok then add 1c. oil. Fry the bamboo shoots for 2 minutes; remove and drain. Remove the oil from the wok. Reheat the wok then add 2 T. oil; stir-fry the black mushrooms until fragrant. Return the bamboo shoots to the wok; add ① cook over medium heat for about 8 minutes, or until the liquid is reduced to half. Add mixture ② to thicken; stir. If only one wok is used, remove mixture to a bowl or plate. Clean the wok.

❸Reheat the wok then add 3 T. oil Put the bok choy and a dash of salt in the wok; stir until the vegetable is hot. Remove and drain. Arrange the bok choy around the platter; place the mushrooms and bamboo shoots in the center and serve.

■See P. 67, Figs.1 and 2 to prepare bok choy.

Fig.1 Cut the bamboo shoots into cone-shaped wedges.

Fig.2 Deep-fry the bamboo shoots until the edges turn golden brown; remove.

蠔油芥蘭 Chinese Broccoli with Oyster Sauce

CANTONESE; SERVES 6

12 stalks Chinese broccoli
   (5-inch lengths)
2 T. oyster sauce
1 T. corn oil

● Bring 1/2 pot of water to a boil; add a dash of salt. Place the Chinese broccoli in the water and cook for 2 minutes. Remove and drain. Place on a serving platter and sprinkle with oyster sauce and 1 T. corn oil. Remove and serve.

Fig.1 Remove the wilted leaves. Use only the tender leaves.

Fig.2 If the stalks are too long, cut them in half after they are cooked

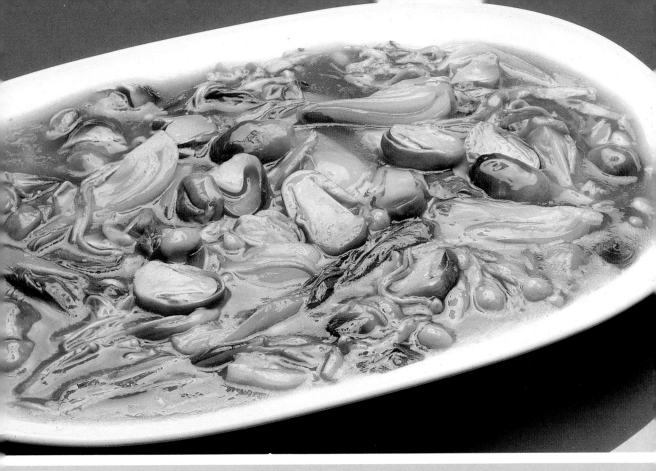

素燴三鮮　Stir-fried Vegetable with Mushrooms

SERVES 6

2/3 lb. bok choy
1 c. canned straw mushrooms
1/2 c. canned enoki mushrooms
1 green onion, cut into 6 pieces

① {
1 T. each: cooking wine or sherry,
              oyster sauce
1/2 t. salt
dash of sesame oil
dash of black pepper
1 c. stock or water
}

② { 1/2 T. cornstarch
1 T. water } mix

❶ Remove only limp leaves from the bok choy. Cut the stalk of bok choy lengthwise into 4 pieces; if very thick cut into 6 pieces. Rinse to clean then blanch in boiling water; remove and plunge in cold water. Set aside for later use.

❷ Heat the wok then add 3 T. oil. Stir-fry the green onions until fragrant. Add all mushrooms; stir briefly then add ① . Cook over high heat until boiling; add bok choy and cook for 3 minutes. Add mixture ② to thicken; stir. Transfer to a serving plate and serve.

Fig.1 If using fresh enoki mushrooms, cut off the hard end before using.

Fig.2 Canned enoki mushrooms may be used.

159

四色素菜　Assorted Vegetable Platter

24 small bok choy
16 oz. canned baby corns
16 oz. canned straw mushrooms
3 fresh tomatoes

① { 4 c. stock
    1 1/2 t. salt

② { 2 t. cornstarch
    1 T. water } mix

1 T. chicken fat

❶ Remove any wilted leaves from the bok choy; trim the stalks to 4-inch lengths. If large bok choy is used, halve or quarter the lengths. Blanch in boiling water; remove, drain, and plunge into cold water. Lightly score an "x" on the non stem end of each tomato. Blanch the tomatoes in boiling water (leavelong enogh so that the skin splits). Remove and peel the tomatoes. Cut each tomato into quarters.

❷ Place 2/3 of ① in a pot and bring it to a boil. Using the same liquid, separately cook bok choy until hot; remove. Separately cook each for 2 minutes then remove: baby corns, mushrooms, and tomatoes. Arrange the vegetables on a serving platters as shown. discard the cooking liquid.

❸ Bring the remaining 1/3 of ① to a boil; add mixture ② to thicken; stir and pour over the vegetables. Sprinkle the melted chicken fat on top; serve.

Fig.1 Lightly score an "x" on the nonstem end of the tomatoes. Blanch the tomatoes in boiling water until the skin splits. Remove and peel.

Fig.2 Cut each tomato in quarters. Lightly flatten the tomatoes so that they can be arranged with the center on the plate.

魚香茄子　Fish-flavored Eggplant

1 lb. eggplant
1 c. oil for frying
2 1/2 oz. ground pork

① {
1 t. hot bean paste
2 T. chopped green onion
1 T. minced ginger root
1 T. minced garlic clove
}

② {
1 1/2 T. soy sauce
3/4 c. stock
1/2 T. each: sugar, white vinegar
dash of cooking wine or sherry
}

③ {
1/2 T. cornstarch
1 T. water
} mix

❶ Cut off the ends of the eggplants. Cut the eggplant into 1/2-inch strips. Heat the wok then add oil. Fry the eggplant strips for about 3 minutes, or until cooked. Remove and drain. Remove the oil from the wok.

❷ Reheat the wok then add 1 T. oil. Stir-fry the ground pork and add ① in order listed, stir after each addition. Return the eggplant to the wok and add ②; cook for 1 minute. Add mixture ③ to thicken; stir. Transfer to a serving plate; serve.

■ Eggplants may be peeled if desired. The oil will be absorbed during the frying process. The oil is released when the eggplant is cooked.

Eggplant in Soy Sauce

1 1/3 lbs. Chinese eggplants
1 1/2 T. minced garlic clove
3 T. oil

① {
3 T. soy sauce
1 T. each: sesame oil,
　　　　　cooking wine
1/2 T. sugar
1/2 c. water
}

❶ Cut the eggplants into 1-inch pieces; soak them in water. Remove and drain them before using.

❷ Heat the wok then add 3 T. oil. Stir-fry the garlic until fragrant; and the eggplant. Stir-fry over high heat for 2 minutes; and ①. Cover and cook for 6 minutes or until the liquid has almost evaporated. Remove and serve.

開洋白菜　Stir-fried Cabbage with Dried Shrimp

SERVES 6

① {
1 1/3 lb. Nappa cabbage
3 T. dried shrimp
1/2 T. each: chopped green onion,
　　　　　minced ginger root
}

② {
1/2 T. cooking wine or sherry
1/2 c. stock
3/4 t. salt
}

③ {
1 1/2 T. cornstarch
2 T. water
} mix

❶ Rinse the cabbage and cut it into 2-inch pieces. Soak the dried shrimp in water until soft; remove and drain.
❷ Heat the wok then add 3 T. oil. Stir-fry ① until fragrant; add cabbage and stir-fry. Add ② and bring to a boil; cover and cook over medium heat for 4 minutes. Add mixture ③ to thicken; stir. Transfer to a serving plate and serve.

Fig.1 Cut the cabbage in half lengthwise.

Fig.2 Cut the cabbage into pieces.

奶油菜胆　Baked Nappa Cabbage and Butter

CANTONESE; SERVES 12

2 2/3 lbs. nappa cabbage
4 oz. sliced pork tenderloin

① { 1 1/2 t. salt
1 t. sugar
2 c. stock

5 T. butter or lard
1/2 c. chopped brown onion
5 T. flour

② { 2 1/2 c. retained cabbage liquid
(retained from step 2)
1/2 c. evaporated milk

❶ Rinse the cabbage and cut it into quarters; cook in boiling water until soft. Remove and drain.
❷ Heat the wok then add 4 T. oil. Stir-fry the sliced pork; add the cabbage and ①. Cook for 5 minutes; remove and drain (retain the liquid). Liquid will be used in ingredients ②. Place the cabbage in a casserole dish. Preheat oven to 450°
❸ Heat the wok then add the butter. Stir-fry the onion until soft; add flour and stir until fragrant. Add ② and stir to make a sauce; pour the sauce over the cabbage. Place the casserole in the oven. Bake casserole for 15 minutes, or until the top is golden brown; remove and serve.
■ This dish may be prepared and set aside then baked just prior to serving.

Fig.1 Melt the butter and remove the scum.

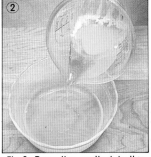

Fig.2 Pour the melted butter into a small bowl; discard residue.

Fig.3 Put the melted butter in the wok; stir-fry the onions and flour.

奶油花菜　Stir-fried Cauliflower in Cream Sauce

CANTONESE;
SERVES 6

① {
1 1/3 lbs. cauliflower
2 c. stock
1 t. salt
dash of rice wine
1/4 c. evaporated milk
}

② {
1 T. cornstarch
1 1/2 T. water
} mix

1 T. butter or corn oil
1 T. chopped ham

❶ Rinse and drain cauliflower; separate flowerets into bite-size pieces. Blanch them in boiling water; remove and drain.

❷ Place ① in a pot and bring to a boil; add cauliflower and cook for 8 minutes, or until the stock is reduced to half. Add milk and mixture ② to thicken; stir. Pour the butter over the cauliflower; transfer the cauliflower to a serving plate. Sprinkle with the chopped ham.

■ For formal use, arrange the flowerets up side down in a bowl; put a plate over the bowl and invert bowl on the plate. Remove the bowl. Pour the cream sauce over the cauliflower.

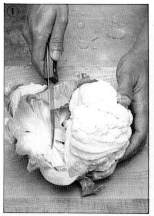 

Fig.1 Rinse and drain the cauliflower. Remove the leaves.

Fig.2 Separate the flowerets into bite-size pieces.

芥末芹菜　Tossed Celery with Mustard Sauce

SERVES 6

2/3 lb. celery hearts

① { 1 T. dry mustard
3/4 T. warm water

② { 3/4 t. salt
1/4 t. sugar
1/2 c. stock or water
1/2 T. cornstarch

❶ Mix ingredients ① in a bowl; cover and set aside. Let stand for 10 minutes. This will be the mustard sauce.

❷ Place ② in a pot and bring to a boil; add the mustard sauce. Stir to mix; set aside for later use.

❸ Cut celery into 2-inch pieces. If ends are very thick, cut lengthwise in half or in thirds. Blanch the celery hearts in boiling water for 30 seconds; remove and drain. Mix with mixture from step ②. Transfer to a serving plate and serve.

Tossed Asparagus with Mustard Sauce

Use the same ingredients as for "Tossed Celery with Mustard Sauce" except substitute 1 lb. asparagus for 2/3 lb. celery hearts.

❶ See steps ❶and ❷of "Tossed Celery with Mustard Sauce" to make the mustard sauce.

❷ Remove the hard skin of the asparagus then cut the asparagus into pieces. Plunge them into boiling water; cook for 3 minutes. Remove and rinse in cold water; drain. Mix the asparagus with mustard sauce; serve.

豆芽雞絲 Stir-fried Shredded Chicken with Bean Sprouts SERVES 6

① {
1/2 lb. chicken meat
1/2 T. cooking wine or sherry
1/4 t. salt
1/2 egg white
3/4 T. cornstarch

1/2 lb. bean sprouts
(remove discolored ends)
1/2 c. oil for frying

② {
1 t. each: cooking wine or sherry,
cornstarch
3/4 t. each: salt, sugar
1 1/2 T. water
dash of black pepper
dash of sesame oil

❶ Shred the chicken meat and mix it with ① . Before frying, add 2 T. oil and mix so that the shredded meat will separate easily during frying.

❷ Heat the wok then add 1/2 c. oil. Stir-fry the chicken shreds and remove (precook). Remove the oil from the wok. Reheat the wok then add 2 T. oil. Stir-fry the bean sprouts, return the shredded chicken to the wok and add ② . Turn the heat to high and quickly stir-fry to mix. Transfer to a serving plate and serve.

Fig.1 Cut off both ends of the bean sprouts.

Fig.2 Rinse the bean sprouts then soak them in water.

涼拌豆芽   **Bean Sprouts Salad**

2 T. dried shrimp
1/2 lb. bean sprouts
   (remove discolored ends)
1/4 c. shredded cooked ham
1/2 c. shredded cucumber
① {
1 t. soy sauce
1/2 t. salt
dash of sugar
1 t. each: sesame oil, white vinegar

❶ Soak the dried shrimp in water until soft; remove and drain. Chop finely. Heat the wok then add 1 T. oil. Stir-fry the shrimp until fragrant. Place ① in a bowl and add the shrimp.

❷ Soak the shredded cucumber in cold water for about 3 minutes; remove and drain. Arrange the shredded cucumber and cooked ham on a serving plate. Blanch the bean sprouts in hot water; remove, drain, and mix with ①. Pour this mixture on top of the cucumber and ham. Toss before serving.

Pickled Nappa Cabbage

2 2/3 lbs. Nappa cabbage
2 T. salt

● Rinse the cabbage and cut it lengthwise into 2 to 4 pieces. Allow it to dry for one day. Sprinkle with salt and put it in a pot. Cover the pot with an airtight lid. Let it stand for two days. Remove the cabbage and rinse it. Cut the cabbage into 1-inch pieces. Sprinkle with sesame oil and soy sauce. Cucumber, choy sum, and rape may be pickled the same way.

涼拌海帶　　Cold Seaweed Salad　　SERVES 6

① 2/3 lb. seaweed strips
1 T. shredded ginger root
1/2 T. each: green onion, cut into strips, shredded hot red pepper
1 T. sesame oil
3/4 T. white vinegar
1 1/3 t. salt

● Cut the seaweed into 3-inch strips and place in boiling water. Bring to a boil then remove and drain. Retain liquid for other uses. Place seaweed strips on a serving plate; pour ① over the seaweed strips. Toss lightly before serving. This salad may be served hot or cold.

■ If dried seaweed is used, it should be soaked in water for 2 hours and the water should be changed often to remove any sliminess. Use 2 oz. dried seaweed because the seaweed expands about five times in bulk.

Fig.1 If using dried seaweed strips, soak them in water for 2 hours. Change the water often to remove any sliminess.
Fig.2 Dried seaweed will expand about five times in bulk after soaking.

麻辣黃瓜　Szechuan Cucumber Slices

1 1/3 lbs. gherkin cucumbers
1/2 T. salt
① { 3 T. shredded ginger root
1 hot red pepper, shredded
3 T. sesame oil
5 dried hot red peppers
1 t. peppercorns
② { 1/4 t. salt
2 T. white vinegar
2 T. sugar

❶ Cut off the ends of the cucumbers. Lengthwise, cut each cucumber into 4 or 6 pieces; cut each piece into 2-inch lengths. Place the pieces of cucumber in a bowl and mix them with salt; let stand for 30 minutes. Place the cucumbers in a colander and rinse them with cold water. Squeeze the pieces of cucumber to remove excess water; transfer to a bowl and add ①.

❷ Heat the wok then add 3 T. sesame oil. Turn the heat to low and stir-fry the dried hot red pepper until fragrant. Add the peppercorns; stir to mix then pour over the cucumbers. Add ② and toss; refrigerate for 6 hours; serve.

Fig.1 Cut the cucumbers lengthwise into 4 to 6 strips and remove the seeds. Cut the cucumber into 2 1/2 inch-strips.

Fig.2 OR use the flat side of the cleaver to flatten the cucumbers then cut it into 2 1/2-inch strips.

薑汁茄子　Eggplant with Ginger Root Sauce

SERVES

1 1/3 lbs. eggplant

① {
2 T. soy sauce
1 t. sesame oil
3 T. minced tender ginger root
}

● Pare and rinse the eggplants; cut them in half lengthwise. Place the eggplant in a pot of boiling water. Turn the heat to medium and cook the eggplant halves for 6 minutes, or until tender. Remove, drain and set aside to cool. When the eggplant is cool, tear the halves lengthwise into strips; place them on a serving plate. Sprinkle mixture ① over the eggplant strips. Serve hot or cold.

■ If the eggplants are tender they do not have to be pared.

Fig.1 Peel and rinse the eggplants. Cut them in half lengthwise and cook them until tender.

Fig.2 When the eggplant is cool, tear it into strips.

香糖核桃　Sweet and Crispy Walnuts

SERVES 6

4 oz. raw, shelled walnuts
3 c. oil for frying
1 T. water
2/3 c. powdered sugar

❶ Heat the wok then add oil. Deep-fry the walnuts for about 1 minute; remove and drain. Remove the oil from the wok and clean it.

❷ Reheat the wok then place the walnuts and 1 T. water in the wok; stir lightly to moisten the walnuts. Add the powdered sugar, stir to mix so that the nuts are lightly coated. Remove the walnuts and place them on a plate to cool; when cool, the sugar will become white and crispy.

■ Roasted walnuts may be used if raw walnuts are unavailable. If roasted walnuts are used omit step ❶. Cashews, peanuts, or almonds may also be used for this dish.

Fig.1 Place the fried walnuts in the wok then add 1 T. water.

Fig.2 Add powdered sugar.

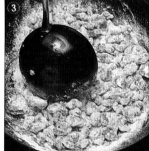

Fig.3 Stir so that all the nuts are completely coated with sugar.

干貝生菜　Stir fried Scallops with Lettuce

SERVES 6

3 dried scallops or
2 T. dried shrimp

① {
3/4 t. salt
dash of black pepper
1 c. stock or water

② {
1 T. cornstarch
1 1/2 T. water
} mix

1 green onion, cut into 6 pieces
1 lb. iceberg lettuce

❶ Place the scallops in a bowl; add 1/2 c. water; soak for 10 hours or steam for 1 hour, or until soft. Remove and drain; retain the liquid. Tear the scallops into shreds. Place the shredded scallops, retained liquid, and ① in a pot; bring to a boil. Add mixture ② to thicken; stir; set aside for later use. Wash the lettuce and tear it into large pieces.

❷ Heat the wok then add 4 T. oil. Stir-fry the onion until fragrant. Add the lettuce and stir-fry it until it is limp. Remove and drain; transfer to the pot of shredded scallops. Place the pot over medium heat; stir to mix. When hot, transfer to a serving platter and serve.

■ If dried shrimp is used, the shrimp must be rinsed and soaked for 20 minutes, or until soft, before using.

Scallops with Bok Choy

● The ingredients and directions are the same as for "Stir-fried Scallops with Lettuce" except substitute 1 2/3 lb. cooked bok choy for lettuce.

千貝三色球　Scallops with Vegetable Balls

PEKING;
SERVES 6

4 dried scallops
carrots   } scooped-out balls
daikon   } combined to
gherkin cucumber } equal 4 cups
① { 1 1/2 c. stock
   { 3/4 t. salt
② { 1 1/2 T. cornstarch } mix
   { 2 T. water

❶ Rinse the scallops and soak them in 1/2 c. of water for 10 hours, or until soft. Remove scallops and retain the liquid. Tear the scallops into shreds.

❷ Place the carrot and daikon balls in a pot; add water to cover. Cook over medium heat for 8 minutes then add the cucumber balls. Cook for 2 minutes; remove the vegetable balls and drain. Discard the water.

❸ Place ①, shredded scallops, retained liquid, and vegetable balls in a deep pot. Cover and cook over medium heat for 10 minutes. Add mixture ② to thicken; stir. Transfer to a serving plate and serve.

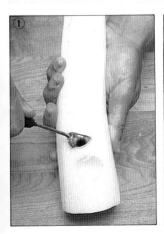 

Fig.1 To make scooped-out balls: Pare the white radish. Press the scooper down to fill the bowl of the scooper.

Fig.2 Turn the scooper in a circular fashion then scoop out the white radish balls.

干扁四季豆　Dried-cooked String Beans

SZECHUAN;
SERVES 6

1 lb. string beans
1 c. oil for frying
1 oz. ground pork
2 T. presoftened dried shrimp, chopped finely
4 T. Szechuan pickled mustard greens, chopped finely

①{
1 T. soy sauce
2 T. water
1 t. sugar
}

1 1/2 T. chopped green onion
1/2 t. sesame oil

❶ Remove the ends of the string beans and pull away any "veiny" strings; rinse and drain. Cut the string beans into 3-inch lengths.

❷ Heat the wok then add oil; turn off the heat. Put the string beans in the wok and turn the heat to medium. Fry for 4 minutes; remove and drain. Remove the oil from the wok. Reheat the wok then add 1T. oil; stir-fry the ground pork until it changes color. Add the shrimp and mustard greens; stir for 30 seconds. Return the string beans to the wok and add ① ; turn the heat to high. Stir quickly to mix. Sprinkle with green onion and sesame oil. Place on a serving plate and serve.

Dried-cooked Bamboo Shoot

● The ingredients and directions are the same as for "Dried-cooked String Beans" except to substitute sliced bamboo shoots for string beans.

蠶豆炒酸菜 Stir-fried Lima Beans with Pickled Mustard Greens   SERVES 6

1/2 lb. pickled mustard greens,
    chopped
3/4 c. cooked lima beans
3/4 c. bamboo shoots, sliced

①
{
1/2 t. salt
1 t. each: soy sauce
       cooking wine or sherry
dash of black pepper
1 T. sesame oil
2 T. water
}

1/2 c. chopped green onion

- Heat the wok then add 2 T.oil. Stir-fry the mustard greens until cooked; remove. Reheat the wok then add 2 T. oil. Stir-fry the lima beans and sliced bamboo shoots; add ① and stir to mix. Return the mustard greens to the wok and add the green onions; stir to mix. Place on a serving plate and serve.
- Dried bean curd may be substituted for the pickled mustard greens. This dish may be served hot or cold.

Spicy Bean Curd Skin

2/3 lb. bean sprouts
1/3 lb. shredded jellyfish
6 sheets (12 inches×6 inches)
    bean curd skins
3 T. sesame oil

① {
1 T. sesame paste
1 1/2 T. soy sauce
1/2 T. each: sugar, vinegar chii oil
1 T. copped green onion
1/2 t. Szechuan peppercorn powder
}
6 sheets (12 inches×6 inches)
    bean curd skins
3 T. sesame oil

❶ Blanch the bean sprouts in boiling water. Remove and plunge in cold water; remove and drain.
❷ Place 1/6 of the bean sprouts and jellyfish on a sheet of bean curd. Roll it up to form a baton-like shape.
❸ Heat the wok then add sesame oil. Fry the bean curd until both sides are golden brown. Remove and cut them into 1-inch rolls. Sprinkle with ①; serve.

175

① { 1 1/3 lbs. beef, for soup
1 each: carrot, potato, brown onion, tomato
1/2 cabbage

② { 1 T. each: cooking wine or sherry
soy sauce
2 t. salt

❶ Cut the beef into 1 1/2-inch pieces. Blanch the beef in boiling water; remove and drain. Transfer the beef to a deep pot; add 12 cups of water and bring to a boil. Turn heat to low and cook for 1 hour, or until the liquid is reduced to three fourth its original amount.

❷ Cut ① into 1/2-inch pieces; cut the cabbage into large squares. Place ① and cabbage in the pot. Cook for 20 minutes over medium heat; add ②. Place in a large bowl and serve.

Fig.1 Cut the onion and tomato into wedges.

Fig.2 Cut the carrot and potato into pieces.

排骨酥湯 Spareribs Soup

TAIWANESE; SERVES 6

1 lb. spareribs

①
- 1 T. each: cooking wine or sherry, soy sauce
- 1/2 T. each: sugar, white vinegar, minced garlic clove
- 1/4 t. salt
- dash of five-spice powder
- 2 T. cornstarch

oil for frying, 8 c. stock

1 1/3 lbs. white radish or taro root

②
- 1 1/2 t. each: cooking wine or sherry, salt
- dash of black pepper, sesame oil
- 2 T. chopped coriander (cilantro)

❶ Cut the spareribs into 1-inch pieces (about 40 total pieces); add ① and mix. Set aside for later use. Heat the wok then add the oil. Deep-fry for 3 minutes, or until golden brown; remove and drain. Transfer to a medium-size heatproof bowl; steam for 30 minutes.

❷ Pare the white radish and cut it into bite-size pieces. Put the white radish and stock in a pot and cook until it is tender. Add ② and stir.

❸ Remove the bowl of spareribs; place a large serving bowl on top of the bowl of spareribs; invert the bowls and remove the steaming bowl. (See P. 32, Figs. 1, 2) Add the stock and white radish to the serving bowl.

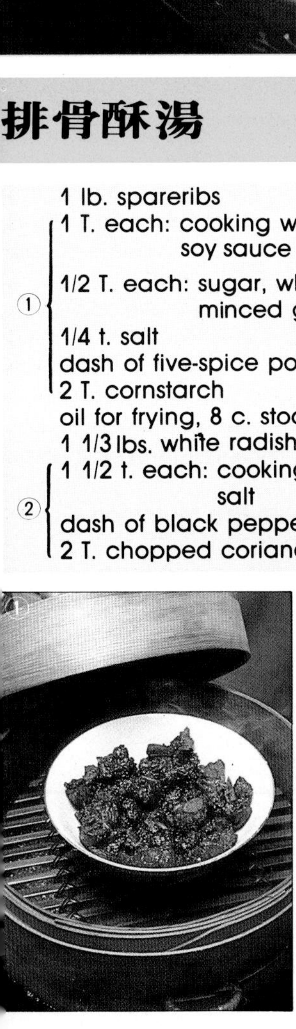

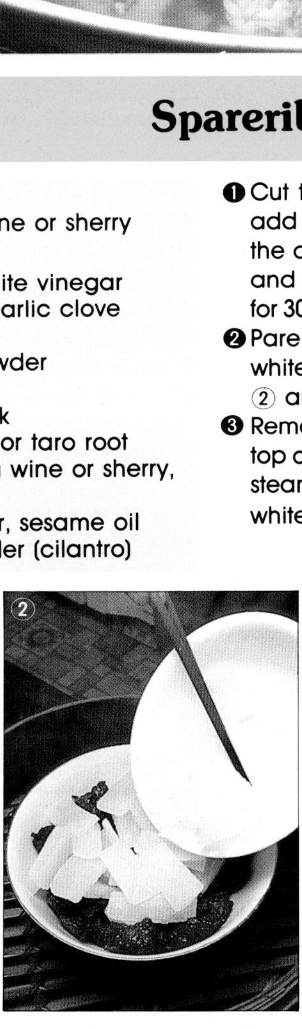

Fig.1 Place the fried spareribs on a medium-size heatproof bowl. Steam for 30 minutes; remove.

Fig.2 If there is enough space in the bowl, fill tee bowl with the precooked white radishes so that the spareribs will remain in place when the bowl is inverted on a serving plate.

冬瓜盅　Eight-treasures Soup in Winter Squash

SERVES 6

1/2 winter squash
(about 7 inches high, 6 2/3 lbs.)

① {
1 c. duckling meat
1/4 c. Chinese black
　　mushroom
2 T. cooked ham
} diced

② {
6 c. stock
1 1/2 t. salt
dash of black pepper
2 T. shredded ginger root
1 T. cooking wine or sherry
}

❶ Cut v-shaped grooves around the top edge of the squash; hollow out the squash. Place the winter squash in boiling water to cover and cook for 20 minutes. Remove and place it in cold water to cool; drain.

❷ Blanch the duckling meat in boiling water; remove and drain. Set aside for later use.

❸ Place ② in a pot and bring to a boil. Pour ① and ② in the squash (the liquid should fill only 90% of the squash). Place the squash in a steamer and steam over medium heat for 1 hour. The winter squash serves as a serving tureen and eaten as a vegetable.

■ Other ingredients such as scallops, button mushrooms, duck gizzards, and lotus seeds may be added to ① .

Stuffed Cucumbers

3 large cucumbers
1/2 lb. ground beef
　　or pork

① {
1/2 t. salt
1 t. sesame oil
1/2 T. cornstarch
}

② {
stock and
retained liquid
from steamed cucumbers
} combined to equal 3/4 cup

1/2 t. salt, 1 t. sesame oil
dash of black pepper
2/3 T. cornstarch

❶ Mix ground beef with ① .

❷ Pare the cucumbers and cut them into 1-inch pieces. Remove the seeds. Sprinkle cornstarch on the inside of the cucumbers; stuff them with meat filling. Steam for 30 minutes; remove to a serving plate.

❸ Boil ② until slightly thickened then pour over the cucumbers.

原盅三味　　Three-flavored Soup　　

① (1) 2 2/3 lbs. winter squash
2 chicken legs
12 slices cooked ham
6 Chinese black mushrooms
3 dried scallops

② (2) 2 1 1/2 inch pieces of green onion
2 slices ginger root
1 T. cooking wine or sherry
6 c. stock or water
1 1/4 t. salt
dash of black pepper

❶ Pare the winter squash and scoop out balls with a melon ball scooper. Cut the chicken legs, through the bone, into bite-size pieces. Blanch the chicken pieces in boiling water, remove, drain, and discard the water. Soak the dried scallops in water for 1 hour; remove and drain.

❷ Place ingredients ① and ② in a casserole; stew over medium heat for 40 minutes. Add the black pepper. Transfer to a serving bowl and serve.

■ The winter squash may be cut into bite-size cubes.

Fig.1 Cut the winter squash into 1-inch square cubes.

Fig.2 Trim the cubes to form round shapes.

火腿瓜夾　Layered Winter Squash Sandwich

SERVES 6

1 length pared winter squash
　(about 1 1/3 lbs.)
24 1 1/2"x1/2" pieces cooked ham
① { 1/2 T. cooking wine or sherry
　　1/4 c. stock
② { 1 1/2 t. salt
　　dash of black pepper
　　dash of sesame oil
　　6 c. stock and retained liquid
　　1 T. shredded ginger root

❶ Trim the winter squash to a rectangular shape (9 1/2"x21/2"and 1 1/4" thick).Place the squash horizontally across a cutting surface. Cut a 1/5 inch slices to 1/4 inch from the bottom (do not cut through the first cut). Continue to cut slices, cutting through every other slice to make a "pocket" (sandwich). Make 24 pairs.

❷ Place the sliced squash in boiling water; cook for 1 minute ; remove and drain. Insert a slice of ham in the pocket of each pair of sliced squash. Arrange the "sandwiches" in a medium-size heatproof bowl by overlapping them. Add ① and steam over high heat for 40 minutes. Remove the bowl of "sandwiches", drain, retain liquid. Include liquid with ingredients ②. Cover the bowl with a serving bowl and invert them (See P. 32, Figs. 1, 2). Remove the steaming bowl. Put② in a pot and bring to a boil; pour into the serving bowl. Sprinkle the ginger root on the squash.

■ When paring the melon, leave a thin layer of green skin for color.

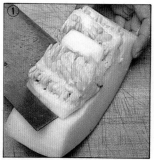

Fig.1 Trim the squash to a rectangular shape 2 1/2 inches wide; remove seeds.

Fig.2 Cut off the skin.

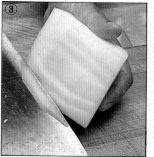

Fig.3 Cut the squash into pieces for easier handling. Cut v-shaped grooves down the length of the squash.

Fig.4 Turn the squash 90 degrees and slice as directed in step ❶.

麻油雞湯　　Sesame Chicken Soup

1 whole chicken (about 2 2/3 lbs.)
4 T. sesame oil
6 slices ginger root
2 c. cooking wine or sherry
① { 5 c. water
2 t. sugar
1 t. salt

❶ Remove any fat from the cavity of the chicken and cut the chicken into bite-size pieces.
❷ Heat the wok then add sesame oil. Stir-fry the ginger root until fragrant; add the pieces of chicken and stir-fry for 1 minute. Add the cooking wine and bring to a boil. Add ① and boil again; turn heat to low and simmer for 20 minutes. Transfer to a serving bowl and serve.
■ The water may be substituted with cooking wine or sherry.

Sesame Pig's Liver

2/3 lb. pig's liver
3 T. black sesame oil
4 slices ginger root
2 c. cooking wine

① { 2 c. water
1/3 t. salt
sugar
2 T. oil

❶ Slice the liver. Heat the wok then add 2 T. oil. Fry the liver on both sides until brown; remove immediately.
❷ Heat the wok then add black sesame oil. Stir-fry the ginger root until fragrant; add cooking wine and ①. Cook for 5 minutes or until boiling; add the liver and bring to a boil. Remove and serve.

川翼洋菇　　Stuffed-Chicken Wing Soup

TAIWANESE;
SERVES 12

16 chicken wings

(1)
[16 1 1/2 inch strips each:
Chinese black mushrooms,
bamboo shoots, cooked ham

2 oz. pork tenderloin

(2)
{ 1 t. soy sauce
{ 1 t. cornstarch

1/2 c. button mushrooms

1 cucumber

(3)
{ 1/2 c. stock, 1/2 t. salt
{ 1/2 t. cooking wine or sherry

(4)
[1 t. salt, 6 c. stock and retained liquid
[dash of sesame oil ·

❶ Cut the wings at the joint. Only the upper part of the wing will be used for this dish. Reserve lower part of wing for other uses. Place the wing parts in a pot of boiling water and cook over low heat for 4 minutes; remove and drain. Set aside to cool. When cool, pull out the bone from the upper wing. Place 1 strip each of ① in the cavity. Slice the pork tenderloin and mix with ②. Blanch in boiling water; when the color changes, remove and drain. Cut the cucumber into bite-size pieces; blanch in boiling water; remove and drain.

❷ In a medium-size, heatproof bowl, arrange the stuffed wings in 3 rows to line the bowl. Place the meat and ③ on top and pack securely. Steam over medium heat for 10 minutes. Remove the bowl and drain the liquid (retain liquid). This liquid will be added to ④. Place a large serving bowl on top of the steaming bowl. Invert the bowls and remove the steaming bowl. (See P. 32, Fig. 1, 2) Add the cucumber and button mushrooms. Bring ④ to a boil; pour into the serving bowl and serve.

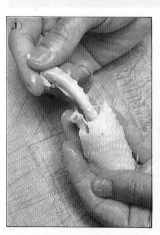 

Fig.1　Remove the bones from the upper wing.

Fig.2　Place a strip each of black mushroom, bamboo shoot, and cooked ham in the cavity.

182

鳳足香菇 Black Mushrooms and Chicken's Feet Soup

CANTONESE; SERVES 6

①
- 6 small Chinese black mushrooms
- 12 chicken feet
- 1 green onion, cut into 6 pieces
- 2 slices ginger root
- 1 T. cooking wine or sherry
- 1 1/2 t. salt
- dash of black pepper
- 6 c. stock

● Declaw the chicken. Remove the main bone (tarsal) from the chicken feet and discard. Cook the chicken feet in boiling water for 1 minute to clean. Remove and rinse in cold water. Place the chicken's feet in a casserole and add ① : stew for 1 hour. Add the Chinese black mushrooms and stew for 15 minutes; serve.

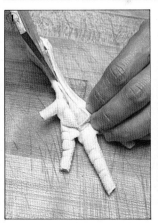

Fig.1 Declaw the chicken. On the bottom of the feet, make a cut down the middle to reveal the main bone (tarsal).

Fig.2 Break the bone at the main joint. Pull out the main bone.

花瓜燉雞 Stewed Chicken with Pickled Cucumbers

TAIWANESE;
SERVES 6

1/2 chicken (about 1 1/3 lbs.)
1/2 c. canned Wei-Chuan pickled
    cucumbers
3 T. pickled cucumber marinade
    (retained from canned
    cucumbers)

① {
1 green onion, cut into 6 pieces
2 slices ginger root
1 T. cooking wine or sherry
1/2 t. salt
6 c. water

- Clean the chicken and cut it into bite-size pieces. Blanch the pieces of chicken in boiling water; remove and transfer to a casserole. Add ① and stew over medium heat for 30 minutes. Add the retained marinade and stew for an additional 10 minutes. Serve.

Stewed Spareribs with Pickled Cucumbers

- Ingredients and directions are the same as for "Stewed Chicken with Pickled Cucumbers" except substitute spareribs for chicken.

當歸鴨湯　　Dang Guei Duckling

TAIWANESE;
SERVES 6

①
- 1 whole duckling (about 3 1/3 lbs.)
- .02 oz. Dang Guei
- 4 T. cooking wine or sherry
- 1 1/4 t. salt
- 6 c. water

● Clean the duckling and cut it into bite-size pieces. Put the pieces of duckling in a pot of boiling water and cook for 5 minutes. Remove and transfer to a casserole. Discard the water. Put ingredients ① in a casserole and stew for 1 hour, or until the duckling meat is tender. Remove and serve.

■ Dang Guei (levisticum) is a type of dry, pungent herb used for flavoring. It is nutritionally beneficial and is available at any Chinese herbal drug store.

Dang Guei Milkfish

- 1 1/3 lbs. milkfish
- 6 c. stock or water

①
- 0.02 oz. Dang Guei
- 1 1/2 T. cooking wine
- 1 1/4 t. salt

● Clean and rinse the milkfish. Cut it diagonally into pieces. Put the fish in a pot of boiling water and cook for 1 or 2 minutes. Remove and transfer to a casserole. Add ① to the casserole and steam for 40 minutes; remove and serve.

185

香菇燉雞 Stewed Chicken with Chinese Black Mushrooms SERVES 6

1 whole chicken (about 2 2/3 lbs.)
12 Chinese black mushrooms
12 slices bamboo shoot

① {
1 T. cooking wine or sherry
1 1/2 t. salt
6 c. water
}

● Cut the chicken into pieces and blanch them in boiling water. Remove the chicken and place it in a casserole; add ① and stew over medium heat for 50 minutes. Add the Chinese black mushrooms and bamboo shoots; continue stewing for another 15 minutes. Remove and serve.

"Silkie" Chicken with Abalone

2 2/3 lbs. "silkie" chicken (dark-boned and dark-skinned chicken)
1 1/3 oz. dried abalone slices

① {
3 c. rice wine
3 c. water
1/2 t. salt
}

● Clean the chicken and blanch it in boiling water. Remove the chicken and place it in a casserole. Add the abalone and ①; stew for 1 1/2 hours; remove and serve while it is still hot.

菊花干貝　Stuffed Egg Flower Soup

TAIWANESE;
SERVES 12

2 dried scallops or 2 T. dried shrimp
2 oz, raw, shelled shrimp
1/2 lb. ground pork

① {
1/2 t. each: cooking wine, salt
1 T. cornstarch, 4 T. water
dash of black pepper, sesame oil
}

2 eggs, for egg sheet, seep p. 79

② {
1/4 c. each: shredded ham,
　　　　　　Chinese black
　　　　　　mushrooms
1/2 c. each: shredded precooked
　　　　　　carrot, bamboo shoots
}

③ {
1 1/2 t. salt, 1 t. cooking wine
dash of: black pepper, sesame oil
6 c. stock
}

❶ Soak the scallops in 1/2 cup of water for 10 hours or steam tor 1 hour. Remove, drain, then tear them into shreds.

❷ Devein and rinse the shrimps; pat dry then chop finely. Mix the shrimp. ground pork, and ① together to make the filling.

❸ Lightly oil a medium-size, heatproof soup bowl. Line the bowl with the egg sheet. (The bowl will be inverted later.) Place the scallops in the center. Neatly arrange 2/3 of ② in a decorative pattern around the scallops. Chop the remaining 1/3 of ② finely and mix it with the filling. Place this mixture on top of the other ingredients and pack securely. Fold the egg sheet to enclose the ingredients. Steam over high heat for 40 minutes. Remove the bowl and drain the liquid. Place a serving bowl on top of the steaming bowl and invert bowls, (See P. 32, Figs. 1, 2) remove the steaming bowl. Make 4 diagonal cuts across the egg sheet, stopping 1 inch from the edge of the egg sheet. Bring ③ to a boil and pour into the serving bowl. Carefully lift the pointed ends of egg sheet to open the "petals"; serve.

■ The diameter of medium size bowl is about 6" (4 cups).

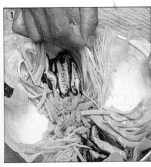

Fig.1 Arrange the ingredients, in order listed, in a medium-size bowl.

Fig.2 Place the filling in the middle of the bowl to cover the other ingredients.

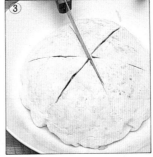

Fig.3 Make 6 to 8 diagonal cuts across the egg sheet, stopping 1 inch from the edge of the egg sheet.

Fig.4 Pour the stock into the bowl. Carefully lift the pointed ends of the egg sheet to open the "petals".

砂鍋魚頭　　Stewed Fish Head Casserole　　SERVES 6

1 fish head (about 1 1/3 lbs.)
1 T. soy sauce
1 stalk fresh garlic or 3 green onions
6 paper-thin slices pork tenderloin
3 Chinese black mushrooms
6 slices bamboo shoot
1 square bean curd, cut into
　bite-size chunks
2/3 lbs. nappa cabbage
2 stalks bok choy
6 slices carrot
1/2 c. presoftened bean threads

① { 1 T. cooking wine or sherry
4 c. stock or water
1 1/2 t. salt

❶ Clean the fish head and pat to dry. Rub 1 T. soy sauce on the fish head and set aside. Cut the fresh garlic into pieces; separate the white and green parts. Cut the cabbage into big pieces. Lengthwise cut the bok choy in half; blanch in boiling water. Remove and drain.

❷ Heat the wok then add 4 T. oil; fry the fish head until both sides are golden brown. Remove. Stir-fry the pork tenderloin; remove. Stir-fry the Chinese black mushrooms; remove. Stir-fry the white garlic pieces and nappa cabbage; remove.

❸ Place the cabbage leaves around the bottom of the casserole. Add the fish head, pork loin, mushrooms, bamboo shoots, bean curd and ① Cook for 3 minutes; remove from heat. Sprinkle green garlic pieces over top and serve.

Stewed Bean Curd Casserole

Use the same ingredients given for "Stewed Fish Head Casserole" but substitute 1 cup shelled shrimp for fish head and use 3 squares of bean curd instead of 1 square.

● Cut the cabbage into pieces and place it around the bottom of the casserole. Add the other ingredients and bring to a boil; remove any scum. Reduce heat to low and cook for 10 minutes.

湯泡魚生　Fish and Vegetable Broth

HUNAN;
SERVES 6

1/2 lb. fillet of fish
2 oz. green vegetable
1 Chinese fried crueller, cut into
　1/2 inch pieces
oil for frying

① {
1/2 T. crushed peanuts or sesame
　　seeds
1 t. each: chopped green onion,
　　sesame oil
dash of black pepper
}

② {
1/2 T. cooking wine or sherry
1 1/2 t. salt
dash of black pepper, white vinegar
6 c. stock
}

❶ Slice the fish meat into paper-thin slices; mix with 1 T. cooking wine. Fry the Chinese fried crueller; remove and set aside for later use.

❷ Place the green vegetable, fried crueller, and ① in a large soup bowl. Place the slices of fish on top of the vegetable, do not overlap the slices of fish. Bring ② to a boil; pour over the fish meat. Use chopsticks to mix the ingredients in the bowl; serve.

■ If Chinese fried crueller is unavailable, substitute crutons, canned button mushrooms, straw mushrooms, or precooked bean threads. Spinach or celery may be used as the green vegetable.

Fig. 1　Slice the Chinese fried crueller into 1/2 inch wide pieces.
Fig. 2　Deep-fry the cruellers; remove and set them aside.

蘿蔔絲魚湯　Fish and White Radish Soup

SZECHUAN;
SERVES 6

1 fish (about 1 2/3 lbs.)
4 T. lard
1 green onion, cut into 6 pieces
6 slices ginger root
1 T. cooking wine or sherry
① { 8 c. water
1 1/2 t. salt
dash of black pepper
3 c. shredded white radish

❶ Clean the fish and pat it dry.
❷ Heat the wok then add the lard. Fry the fish on both sides until golden brown; move the fish aside. Stir-fry the green onion and ginger root until fragrant. Add ① and shredded white radish. Return the fish to the center of the wok; cook for 15 minutes over high heat. Sprinkle with black pepper; remove and serve.
■ This dish may be served as two dishes. The fish may be served separately by removing it from the broth. Sprinkle with chopped ginger root and chopped garlic, soy sauce, and white vinegar before serving. The soup may be served in bowls.
■ Carp or spotted grouper may be used for this dish.

Fig.1 Remove the fish from the broth and place it on a serving platter.

Fig.2 Sprinkle with chopped ginger root and chopped garlic, soy sauce, and white vinegar.

190

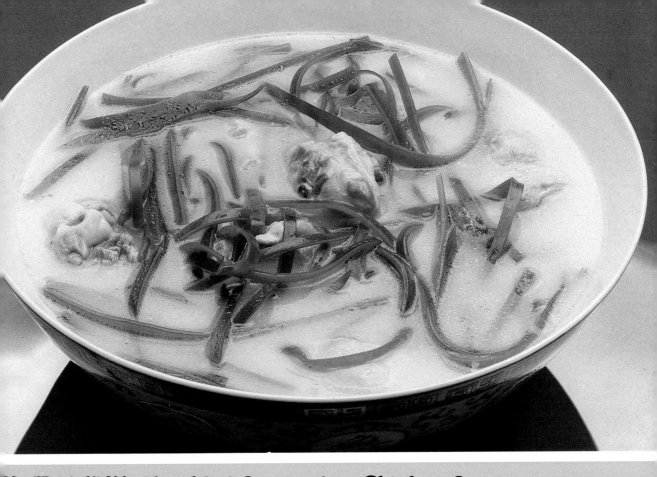

海帶絲雞湯 Shredded Seaweed in Chicken Soup

SERVES 6

① {
1/2 lb.presoaked shredded seaweed
2 chicken legs, cut into bite-size pieces
7 c. water
1 T. cooking wine or sherry
1 1/2 t. salt
1 1/2 T. shredded ginger root
1 T. evaporated milk
}

● Make several cuts into the mass of presoaked seaweed to shorten the lengths. Blanch the chicken legs in boiling water; remove then rinse them under cold water to clean them thoroughly. Place the seaweed and chicken legs in a large pot. Add the water and bring it to a boil; remove any scum. Cover and cook over low heat for 20 minutes. Add ① ; test for saltiness. Add the milk (The milk is added for color; however, it may be omitted.). Transfer to a large serving bowl; serve.

■ The chicken legs may be substituted with spareribs. Daikon (white radish) or bean curd may be added.

■ If dried seaweed is used, it must be presoaked (see p. 19).

Seaweed in Sparerib and Bean Curd Soup

1 c. knotted seaweed
1 lb. spareribs, cut into bite-size pieces
2 squares bean curd, cut into bite-size pieces
7 c. water
① { same as ingredients in ① of "Shredded Seaweed in Chicken Soup"

❶ Blanch the spareribs in boiling water; remove and discard the water.
❷ Put the spareribs and seaweed in 7 cups of boiling water; bring to a boil. Remove any scum. Cook over low heat for 40 minutes. Add bean curd and ① ; bring to a boil.

191

番茄排骨湯　Tomato and Sparerib Soup

SERVES 6

- 2/3 lb. spareribs
- ① { 1 T. cooking wine or sherry
      9 c. water
- ② { 2 whole tomatoes
      1/2 c. canned button mushrooms
      1 1/2 t. salt
      dash of black pepper

❶ Cut the spareribs into bite-size pieces; blanch in boiling water; remove and drain. Lightly score an "x" on the skin of the non-stem end of the tomatoes. Blanch the tomatoes in boiling water; remove then peel. Coarsely dice the tomatoes. Slice the button mushrooms.

❷ Bring ① to a boil; add the spareribs and cook over low heat for 40 minutes. Add ②; cook for 5 minutes. Transfer to a large serving bowl and serve.

Tomato and Egg Soup

- 1 c. tomato, peeled and cut into pieces
- 3 eggs, beaten
- Nappa cabbage or spinach, cut into pieces 2 inches long
- ① { 1 1/2 t. salt
      dash of black pepper
      sesame oil
      6 c. stock

● Bring ① to a boil. Add tomato and cook until soft. Add the beaten eggs in a thin stream; cook until the eggs surface to the top. Add the cabbage. Transfer to a serving bowl; serve.

洋菇鶉蛋湯　Mushrooms and Quail Egg Soup

CANTONESE;
SERVES 6

12 quail eggs
12 leaves coriander (cilantro)
1 T. chopped cooked ham
① { 12 slices each: bamboo shoots, pre-
　　　cooked carrot, cooked ham
12 straw mushrooms
12 stalks rape greens

1/2 T. cooking wine or sherry
1 1/2 t. salt
② { dash of black pepper
dash of sesame oil
6 c. stock

❶ Coat 12 Chinese soup spoons with oil; break an egg into each spoon. At one end of the bowl of the spoon, place a leaf of coriander. Sprinkle some chopped ham at the opposite end of the leaf of coriander. Steam over low heat for 3 minutes; remove the spoons. When the eggs are cool remove them from spoons.

❷ Separately blanch ingredients in ① ; remove to a large soup bowl. Place the steamed eggs in the soup bowl. Bring ② to a boil then pour it into the soup bowl; serve.

ig.1　Grease a spoon or small plate with oil.

ig.2　Break an egg into each spoon.

ig.3　Place a leaf of coriander at one end of the bowl of the spoon.
　　　Sprinkle some chopped ham at the opposite end of the coriander; steam over low heat.

193

鮑魚豬肚湯 Abalone and Pork Maw Soup

TAIWANESE
SERVES 12

1/2 1-lb. can abalone
1/2 precooked pork maw
1/2 lb. pickled mustard greens

① 1/2 c. stock
1/4 t. salt

6 c. stock and retained liquid
② dash of salt
dash of sesame oil
1 t. cooking wine or sherry

❶ Slice the abalone, pork maw, and pickled mustard greens into thin slices.
❷ Arrange the abalone slices, by slightly overlapping them, to line the center of a medium-size bowl. Arrange the slices of pork maw around the slices of abalone. Place the pickled mustard greens and any end pieces of pork maw and abalone in the center to fill the bowl. Pack tightly and add ①. Steam over medium heat for 15 minutes.
❸ Remove the bowl from the steamer. Place a plate on the bowl and tilt them slightly to drain the liquid (retain liquid). Add the retained liquid to ②. Place a large serving bowl on the steaming bowl; invert the bowls and remove the steaming bowl (See P.32, Figs. 1, 2). Bring ② to a boil then pour it into the soup bowl; serve.
■ To prepare pork maw, See P. 96.

Fig.1 Arrange the abalone slices in the center of a medium-size bowl by slightly overlapping them in a circular fashion.

Fig.2 Arrange the sliced pork maw next to the slices of abalone to cover the edges of the bowl. Fill the center of the bowl with pickled mustard greens and any end pieces of pork maw and abalone.

排骨豆芽湯　**Bean Sprout and Sparerib Soup**　SERVES 6

1/2 lb. spareribs
1 small tomato
1/2 lb. bean sprouts
① { 9 c. water
2 slices ginger root
1 1/2 t. salt

❶ Cut the spareribs into bite-size pieces; blanch them in boiling water, remove and drain. Lightly score an "x" on the non-stem end of the tomato. Blanch the tomato in boiling water; remove and peel. Cut the tomato in half crosswise; gently squeeze the halves to remove the seeds then dice them.

❷ Bring ① to a boil; add the spareribs and cook over low heat for 40 minutes.

❸ Heat the wok then add 2 T. oil. Add the tomato and 1 T. soy sauce; stir to mix; and add to the spareribs. Add bean sprouts and salt to spareribs. Cook for 20 minutes. Remove to a serving soup bowl.

Stuffed Bean Curd Soup

12 pieces stuffed bean curd (see steps ❶ and ❷, p. 130)
① { 1 T. cooking wine
1 1/2 t. salt
dash of black pepper
dash of sesame oil
6 c. stock
green vegetable
coriander

● Bring ① to a boil. Add the stuffed bean curd and cook over low heat for 6 minutes or until the bean curd is cooked. Add vegetable and coriander; bring to a boil; remove and serve.

黃瓜細粉湯 Sliced Cucumber and Bean Thread Soup SERVES 6

12 slices lean meat (pork, beef, or chicken)

① 1 t. each: cooking wine or sherry, soy sauce
2 t. cornstarch

② 6 c. stock
3/4 t. salt

1 1.7 oz. pkg. bean threads
12 thin slices Szechuan pickled mustard greens
12 thin slices cucumber

③ 1 T. each: chopped green onions, soy sauce
dash of black pepper, sesame oil

❶ Mix the meat with ①; set aside for later use. Soak the bean threads in water, to cover, until soft. Remove, drain, and cut in half. Soak the Szechuan pickled mustard greens in water for 20 minutes; remove and drain.

❷ Bring ② to a boil; add bean threads; bring to a boil. Separately add the pieces of meat one by one. Add pickled mustard greens and cucumber slices. Turn off the heat. Put ③ in a serving soup bowl; pour the soup into the soup bowl; serve.

■ After pickled mustard greens and cucumber have been added to the soup, the heat must be turned off immediately to prevent the vegetables from overcooking. (They should be crunchy.)

Fig.1 Soak the bean threads in water until soft; remove.

Fig.2 Cut the bean threads into 4 inch lengths.

榨菜肉絲湯 Mustard Greens and Pork Loin Soup

SERVES 6

① 3 oz. pork loin
1/2 t. cooking wine or sherry
1/8 t. salt
1/2 T. water
1 t. cornstarch

② 6 c. stock
dash of salt
dash of black pepper
dash of sesame oil

1/2 c. bamboo shoots, shredded
1/2 c. Szechuan pickled mustard
　　greens, shredded
1 T. chopped green onion

❶ Shred the pork loin and mix with ① . Set aside for later use.
❷ Soak the shredded Szechuan pickled mustard greens in water for 2 minutes; remove and squeeze out the water.
❸ Bring ② to a boil; add bamboo shoots and shredded meat. Stir lightly to separate the shreds; bring to a boil again. Add the Szechuan pickled mustard greens and chopped green onion; transfer to a serving soup bowl; serve.

Fig.1　Slice the Szechuan pickled mustard greens.

Fig.2　Place the slices in a small stack and then shred them.

Fig.3　Soak the mustard greens in water for 2 minutes to remove the salty taste. Squeeze out excess water.

197

酸菜肚絲湯 Pork Maw with Pickled Mustard Greens Soup

TAIWANESE;
SERVES 6

1 c. pork maw
1 c. pickled mustard greens } shredded
1/2 c. canned shredded bamboo shoots

① { 6 c. chicken stock or water
salt, to taste
dash of sesame oil

● Bring ① to a boil; add pork maw, pickled mustard greens, and bamboo shoots. Bring to a boil; turn the heat to low and cook for 5 minutes. Transfer to a large serving bowl and serve.

■ For directions to prepare pork maw, see page 96.
■ The saltiness of pickled mustard greens will vary depending upon the manufacturer. Taste before adding salt.

Duckling with Pickled Mustard Greens Soup

1/2 duckling
1 1/2 c. pickled mustard cabbage cut in pieces
① { 7 c. water
1 T. cooking wine
② { sesame oil
dash of black pepper
1 T. ginger root

❶ Clean the duckling and cut it into pieces. Blanch the duckling in boiling water then remove it.
❷ Bring ① to a boil; add the duckling and pickled mustard greens. Bring to a boil; turn the heat to low and cook for 40 minutes. Add ②. Salt to taste.

198

三鮮干絲湯 **Three-flavored Shredded Bean Curd Soup** SERVES 6

① {
1/3 c. shredded Chinese black
    mushrooms
1/2 c. canned shredded bamboo
    shoots
1/3 c. shredded cooked ham
1 1/2 c. shredded white pressed
    bean curd
}

② {
1 T. cooking wine or sherry
1 1/2 t. salt
dash of black pepper
6 c. stock or water
1 t. sesame oil
}

- Bring ② to a boil; add ① . Turn heat to low and cook for 5 minutes. Transfer to a large serving bowl and serve.
- ■ This soup is delicious and very simple to prepare. It is suitable for family use as well as for banquets.

Fig.1 Slice the white pressed bean curd.

Fig.2 Slightly overlap the slices then shred them.

肉羹   **Pork and Fish Paste Soup**

TAIWANESE;
SERVES 6

4 oz. pork loin, cut into paper-thin,
    bite-size pieces

① { 1 T. each: cornstarch, soy sauce
    2 T. chopped, sauteed shallots

4 oz. fish paste

② { 6 c. water
    1 t. each: salt, sugar
    1/4 c. Chinese black
       mushrooms   } shredded
    1 c. bamboo shoots

③ { 6 T. water
    4 T. cornstarch } mix

④ { 1 T. soy sauce, 2 t. white vinegar
    dash of black pepper, sesame oil
    dash of chopped coriander

❶ Mix the pieces of meat and ① together. Add fish paste and mix thoroughly. Each piece should be completely coated with fish paste.

❷ Bring ② to a boil. Separately add pork slices; bring to a boil. Add mixture ③ to thicken; stir. Turn off the heat and add ④. Transfer to a serving soup bowl; serve.

■ **To prepare fish paste:** Clean the fish meat and chop it finely. Transfer it to a bowl and stir. When it becomes sticky it is ready for use. Ready-made fish paste may be purchased.

Fig.1 Mix the pieces of meat and ① together. Add fish paste and mix thoroughly.

Fig.2 Put the coated pork slices in boiling soup piece by piece.

Fig.3 Cook until the pork slices surface to the top; remove.

黄魚羹 　　Yellow Fish Soup

CANTONESE;
SERVES 6

① 1/2 lb. diced yellow fish meat
1 c. soft bean curd, diced
3/4 c. each: diced bamboo shoots, sliced button mushrooms
1/4 c. each: cooked ham (cut into small pieces), precooked green peas

② 1 1/2 t. salt, 6 c. stock
dash of black pepper
dash of cooking wine or sherry
dash of sesame oil

③ 5 T. cornstarch ⎱ mix
6 T. water ⎰

④ 2 egg whites ⎱ beaten
2 T. water ⎰

- Bring ② to a boil; add ①. Add fish and stir lightly to separate. Bring to a boil and pour mixture ③ to thicken; stir. Slowly pour ④ while stirring. Turn off the heat. Transfer to a serving bowl and serve.

■ If a whole fish is used, steam the fish then remove the meat and use it for this dish.

■ If used for family, whole eggs may be used. Dried scallops and / or pork tendons may be added for banquet use.

■ A hot and sour taste may be obtained by adding soy sauce, white vinegar, sesame oil, black pepper, coriander, green onions, and ginger root.

Fig.1 Cut the fish meat in small pieces.

Fig.2 Prepare the soft bean curd, bamboo shoots, button mushrooms, ham and green peas as directed.

太極青雲　　Green Pea and Corn Soup

① { 1 1 lb. can creamed corn
　　4 c. stock
　　1 t. salt

② { 1 c. green peas, pureed
　　2 c. stock　　} blended
　　1/2 t. salt

③ { 4 T. cornstarch } mix
　　5 T. water

❶ Bring ① to a boil Add 2/3 of mixture ③ to thicken; stir. Pour into a large serving bowl.

❷ Bring ② to a boil. Add remaining 1/3 of mixture ③ to thicken; stir. Slowly pour into one side of the serving bowl. Use a spoon to arrange the mixture to produce the design shown. (The mixture of green peas is on the surface of the corn.)

Fig.1　Pour the corn soup into a large serving bowl.

Fig.2　Slowly pour the green pea soup on one side of the serving bowl and ladle the mixture carefully to produce the design shown.

三絲魚翅 **Shark's Fin Soup** TAIWANESE; SERVES 12

① 1/2 lb. presoftened shark's fin
   1/2 lb. presoftened fish skin
   1 green onion, cut into 6 pieces
   6 slices ginger root
   1 T. cooking wine or sherry
   3 c. water

② 6 c. stock
   1 c. bamboo shoots
   1/2 c. pork tenderloin } shredded
   4 T. black mushrooms
   2 T. ham
   1 T. cooking wine or sherry
   3 T. soy sauce
   1/2 t. each: salt, sugar, sesame oil

③ 5 T. cornstarch } mix
   6 T. water
   1 T. white vinegar, 1 T. shredded ham

❶ Heat the wok then add 1 T. oil. Stir-fry the green onion and ginger root until fragrant. Add 1 T. cooking wine and 3 c. water. Remove onion and ginger root from the wok. Add the shark's fin and fish skin; cook for 5 minutes. Remove and drain (discard liquid).

❷ Bring 6 c. stock in ② to a boil. Add remaining ingredients in ② Add shark's fin and fish skin; cook for 6 minutes over medium heat, or until the shark's fin is soft. Add mixture ③; stir to thicken. Add 1 T. vinegar and a dash of black pepper. Transfer ingredients to a large serving bowl. sprinkle the shredded ham on top of the soup.

■ If fish skin is unavailable, substitute by increasing shark's fin to 1 lb. See p. 18 for method to presoften.

■ Precooked nappa cabbage leaves may be used to line the serving bowl before pouring the soup in the bowl.

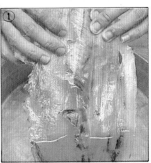  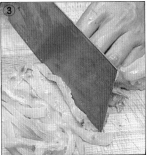

Fig.1 Soak the fish skin in hot water for 6 hours; remove the fish. Discard the water. Add fresh water and cook over low heat until the fish skin is soft. Remove and plunge the skin in cold water.
Fig.2 Remove the residue from the surface of the skin.
Fig.3 Shred the fish skin.

魚翅燒雞　**Braised Chicken with Shark's Fin**　TAIWANESE; SERVES 12

1 whole chicken (about 2 lbs.)
2 T. soy sauce
oil for frying
1 green onion, cut into 6 pieces
6 slices ginger root
1 T. cooking wine or sherry
4 oz. presoftened shark's fin
4 oz. presoftened fish skin } shredded

① {
1 c. bamboo shoots
2 T. each. black mushrooms, ham } shredded
6 c. stock
1/2 t. salt, 1 T. cooking wine or sherry
3 T. soy sauce, dash of sugar

② {
3 T. cornstarch
4 T. water } mix

dash of white vinegar, black pepper

❶ Wash the chicken and pat it dry. Rub the chicken with soy sauce. Heat the wok then add oil. Deep-fry the chicken over high heat until golden brown; remove and drain.

❷ Reheat the wok then add 1T. oil. Stir-fry the green onion and ginger root until fragrant. Add 1T. cooking wine and 3 c. water. Bring to a boil, remove onion and ginger root from the wok. Add the shark's fin and fish skin; cook over medium heat for 5 minutes. Remove; drain liquid (discard).

❸ Bring stock in ① to a boil. Add remainder of ①. Add the chicken; cover. Cook over medium heat for 30 minutes. Add shark's fin and fish skin; cook for 5 minutes. Remove the chicken to a serving casserole; add mixture ② to thicken the soup; stir. Add the vinegar and black pepper. Pour into the serving casserole; serve.

■ If fish skin is unavailable, substitute by increasing the amount of shark's fin. See p. 18 for method to presoften.

Fig.1　Place the fin sheet in a bowl and add boiling water. Soak for 1 hour then remove it. Add water and bring to a boil. Turn off the heat. Soak for at least 1 hour.

Fig.2　The fin is ready to use when the skin is soft and has expanded.

蟹肉燕窩羹　Crab Meat and Bird's Nest Soup

SERVES 12

① 1 oz. bird's nest

① { 1 c. stock
1/4 t. salt

② { 1/2 T. cooking wine or sherry
1 1/2 t. salt
dash of sesame oil
6 c. stock

1/2 c. crab meat

③ { 5 T. cornstarch
6 T. water } mix

④ { 2 egg whites
2 T. water } beat together

❶ Select a bird's nest that is white with no feathers. Place the bird's nest in 6 cups hot water. Soak for 1 day ; remove the nest and let it drain. Remove any remaining feathers.

❷ Steam the bird's nest with ① for 30 minutes over medium heat. Remove the bird's nest then cook with ② in pot; bring ingredients to a boil. Add the crab meat and mixture ③ to thicken; stir. Turn off the heat and slowly pour beaten mixture ④ into the bowl. Stir lightly to mix. Transfer to a serving bowl and serve.

Fig.1　Select a bird's nest that is white with no feathers. Soak the nest in hot water for 1 day.

Fig.2　Remove the bird's nest when it has expanded; remove any remaining feathers.

205

味全企業股份有限公司 **wei-chuan u.s.a. inc.**
味全股份有限公司 **wei-chuan company inc.**

鼎爐傳香

中國，是個有著豐沛文
化遺產的民族，而這深遠
的文化，表現在生活上，
最顯著處莫過於飲食。

飲食，在中國不僅僅是
生活的需要，經過了多少
年來的蘊涵，世代相傳成
爲一門精緻的藝術。

30年來，味全本著服務
人群的精神，致力於食品
的開發研究，以科學的方
法，精湛的調味技藝，保
存了中國飲食特有的風味
，不但滿足了人們的口福
，並將中國烹調的精髓發
揚光大，成爲一支生生不
息的"香火。

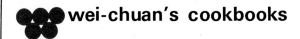 **wei-chuan's cookbooks**

A

Series of Books

for Your

Pleasure

and Enjoyment

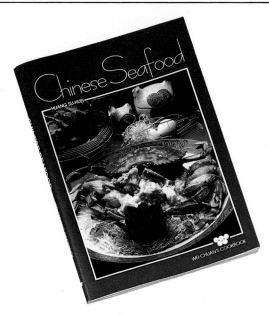

CHINESE SEAFOOD

This book contains 127 recipes that represent a wide variety of seafood. The book includes full-color photographs of most of the dishes and the directions are easy to follow. By using this book, you can become familiar with the preparation of Chinese Seafood and enjoy the dishes served at famous restaurants. The book is 7¼"x10¼", 108 pages, softbound, and is encased in a clear plastic cover. It is published in two editions, English and Chinese.

CHINESE APPETIZERS AND GARNISHES

This specialty book includes basic, popular, assorted, and elegant appetizer platters. The garnish section features adaptable and special garnishes. Small step-by-step, full-color photographs enable you to pepare garnishes and appetizers for all occasions. The softbound book has 164 pages and measures 7¼"x10¼". Each book is encased in a clear plastic cover. CHINESE APPETIZERS AND GARNISHES is published in Chinese/English (bilingual).

CHINESE COOKING FOR BEGINNERS

The directions in this book are simple and clearly written for the neophyte cook. It contains recipes for 89 tasty dishes and 10 delicious snacks. Most of the recipes include small step-by-step photographs in full color. Its mouth-watering, full-color photographs also appeal to expert cooks. The book is 7¼"x10¼", 104 pages, softbound, and is encased in a clear plastic cover. It is published English and Chinese.

CHINESE CUISINE

This book contains a selection of 179 recipes that represent a wide variety of Chinese food. The recipes are practical and not difficult to prepare. This 7¼"x10¼", 208 page book includes full-color photographs of the dishes and has a soft cover that is encased in a clear plastic cover. It is published in English and Chinese/English(bilingual). Small step-by-step photographs are added in English edition. The hardbound edition is published in Japanese and French.

CHINESE CUISINE II

Small photographs that show the step-by-step procedures of the 187 recipes and 50 practical and simple garnishes are combined in this book. The book is 7¼"x10¼", hardbound, and is printed in Chinese/English (bilingual).

CHINESE SNACKS

Chinese Snacks is a collection of 185 kinds of famous snacks from various regions of China. All the recipes include small step-by-step photographs in full color. The 7¼"x10¼", 198 page book is available in soft and hard covers. The softbound book is encased in a clear plastic cover. It is published in Chinese/English(bilingual). The hardbound edition is published in Japanese.

MEDITATIONS ON NATURE

This artistically designed book contains full-color photographs and ink sketches that will help you learn the art of flower arrangement more easily. This book is indispensable in adding beauty to your life and daily environment It is printed in Chinese/English, hardbound, 184 pages, and is 7¼"x10¼".

味全烹飪教室
CHINESE COOKING MADE EASY
YOU ARE WELCOME
TO ENROLL

Chinese Cuisine

WEI-CHUAN'S COOK BOOK

Author Huang Su-Huei
Published by Wei-Chuan's Cooking
Distributed by Wei-Chuan Publishing Co., Ltd.
2nd F1., Section 4, Jen Ai Rd.
Taipei, Taiwan, R. O. C.
Tel: 702-1148 · 702-1149 · 704-2729

Wei-Chuan's Cooking
844 Ridgeside Dr.,
Monterey Park, CA.91754
Tel: (818) 289-8288 • 576-7511

First Printing January 1972. Printed 10
Enlarged Printing October 1974. Printed 9.9.1
Revised Printing May 1976. Printed C1. 36
Enlarged First Popular Printing May 1983.
C7 Printing September 1985

Colour Separated by: International Scanner Colour Separation Inc.